I0164768

Doggin' Philadelphia

The 50 Best Places To Hike With Your Dog In The Delaware Valley

DOUG GELBERT

illustrations by

ANDREW CHESWORTH

CRUDEN BAY BOOKS

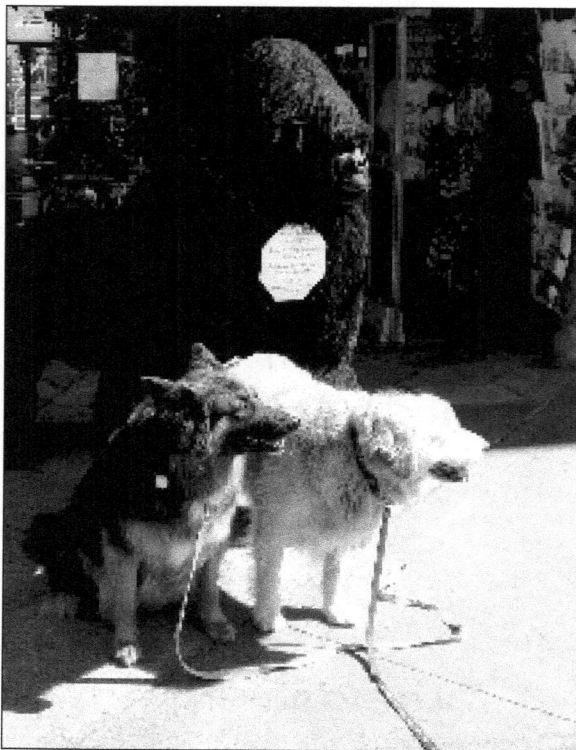

There is always a new trail to look forward to...

DOGGIN' PHILADELPHIA: THE 50 BEST PLACES TO HIKE
WITH YOUR DOG IN THE DELAWARE VALLEY

Copyright 2013 by Cruden Bay Books

All rights reserved. No part of this book may be reproduced or
transmitted in any form or by any means, electronic or mechanical,
including photocopying, recording or by any information storage and
retrieval system without permission in writing from the Publisher.

Cruden Bay Books
PO Box 467
Montchanin, DE 19710
www.hikewithyourdog.com

International Standard Book Number 978-1-935771-23-4

*"Dogs are our link to paradise...to sit with a dog on a hillside
on a glorious afternoon is to be back in Eden,
where doing nothing was not boring - it was peace."*
- Milan Kundera

Ahead On The Trail

The Best Of The Best   12

No Dogs!   15

Best Places - Pennsylvania   17

Best Places - Delaware   87

Best Places - New Jersey   107

Your Dog At The Beach   122

Philadelphia Area Parks By Location   128

Also...

Hiking With Your Dog   5

Outfitting Your Dog For A Hike   8

Low Impact Hiking With Your Dog   11

Introduction

Philadelphia can be a great place to hike with your dog. Within an hour's drive you can hike on sand trails, climb hills that leave you panting, walk on some of the most historic grounds in America, explore the estates of America's wealthiest families or circle lakes for seven miles and never lose sight of the water.

Sometimes the best canine hike comes by parking beside an old forest jeep road and disappearing with your dog for hours of solitude in the woods. I have sought out more formal day-hiking fare and selected what I consider to be the 50 best places to take your dog for an outing in the Delaware Valley according to subjective criteria including the variety of hikes available, opportunities for canine swimming and pleasure of the walks. Included are a mix of parks that feature long walks and parks that contain short walks; at the end are rules for dogs at the beach. Did I miss your favorite? Let us know at *hikewithyourdog. com.*

For dog owners it is important to realize that not all parks are open to our best trail companions (see page 15 for a list of parks that do not allow dogs). It is sometimes hard to believe but not everyone loves dogs. We are, in fact, in the minority when compared with our non-dog owning neighbors.

So when visiting a park always keep your dog under control and clean up any messes and we can all expect our great parks to remain open to our dogs. And maybe some others will see the light as well. *Remember, every time you go out with your dog you are an ambassador for all dog owners.*

Grab that leash and hit the trail!
DBG

Hiking With Your Dog

So you want to start hiking with your dog. Hiking with your dog can be a fascinating way to explore the Philadelphia region from a canine perspective. Some things to consider:

🐾 Dog's Health

Hiking can be a wonderful preventative for any number of physical and behavioral disorders. One in every three dogs is overweight and running up trails and leaping through streams is great exercise to help keep pounds off. Hiking can also relieve boredom in a dog's routine and calm dogs prone to destructive habits. And hiking with your dog strengthens the overall owner/dog bond.

🐾 Breed of Dog

All dogs enjoy the new scents and sights of a trail. But some dogs are better suited to hiking than others. If you don't as yet have a hiking companion, select a breed that matches your interests. Do you look forward to an entire afternoon's hiking? You'll need a dog bred to keep up with such a pace, such as a retriever or a spaniel. Is a half-hour enough walking for you? It may not be for an energetic dog like a border collie. If you already have a hiking friend, tailor your plans to his abilities.

🐾 Conditioning

Just like humans, dogs need to be acclimated to the task at hand. An inactive dog cannot be expected to bounce from the easy chair in the den to complete a 3-hour hike. You must also be physically able to restrain your dog if confronted with distractions on the trail (like a scampering squirrel or a pack of joggers). Have your dog checked by a veterinarian before significantly increasing his activity level.

🐾 Weather

Hot humid summers do not do dogs any favors. With no sweat glands and only panting available to disperse body heat, dogs are much more susceptible to heat stroke than we are. Unusually rapid panting and/or a bright red tongue are signs of heat exhaustion in your pet.

Always carry enough water for your hike. Even the prime hiking days of late fall through early spring that don't seem too warm can cause discomfort in dark-coated dogs if the sun is shining brightly. During cold snaps, short-coated breeds may require additional attention.

🐾 Trail Hazards

Dogs won't get poison ivy but they can transfer it to you. Some trails are littered with small pieces of broken glass that can slice a dog's paws. Nasty thorns can also blanket trails that we in shoes may never notice.

🐾 Ticks

You won't be able to spend much time in Delaware Valley woods without encountering ticks. All are nasty but the deer tick - no bigger than a pin head - carries with it the spectre of Lyme disease. Lyme disease attacks a dog's joints and makes walking painful. The tick needs to be embedded in the skin to transmit Lyme disease. It takes 4-6 hours for a tick to become embedded and another 24-48 hours to transmit Lyme disease bacteria.

When hiking, walk in the middle of trails away from tall grass and bushes. And when the summer sun fades away don't stop thinking about ticks - they remain active any time the temperature is above 30 degrees. By checking your dog - and yourself - thoroughly after each walk you can help avoid Lyme disease. Ticks tend to congregate on your dog's ears, between the toes and around the neck and head.

🐾 Water

Surface water, including fast-flowing streams, is likely to be infested with a microscopic protozoa called *Giardia*, waiting to wreak havoc on a dog's intestinal system. The most common symptom is crippling diarrhea. Algae, pollutants and contaminants can all be in streams, ponds and puddles. If possible, carry fresh water for your dog on the trail - your dog can even learn to drink happily from a squirt bottle.

❧ Rattlesnakes and Copperheads, etc.

Rattlesnakes and their close cousins, copperheads, are not particularly aggressive animals but you should treat any venomous snake with respect and keep your distance. A rattler's colors may vary but they are recognized by the namesake rattle on the tail and a diamond-shaped head. Unless cornered or teased by humans or dogs, a rattlesnake will crawl away and avoid striking. Avoid placing your hand in unexamined rocky areas and crevasses and try and keep your dog from putting his nose in such places as well. Stick to the trail and out of high grass where you can't see well. If you hear a nearby rattle, stop immediately and hold your dog back. Identify where the snake is and slowly back away.

If you or your dog is bitten, do not panic but get to a hospital or veterinarian with as little physical movement as possible. Wrap between the bite and the heart. Rattlesnakes might give "dry bites" where no poison is injected, but you should always check with a doctor after a bite even if you feel fine.

❧ Porcupines

Porcupines are easy for a curious dog to catch and that makes them among the most dangerous animals you may meet because an embedded quill is not only painful but can cause infection if not properly removed.

Outfitting Your Dog For A Hike

These are the basics for taking your dog on a hike:

- **Collar.**
  A properly fitting collar should not be so loose as to come off but you should be able to slide your flat hand under the collar.

- **Identification Tags.**
  Get one with your veterinarian's phone number as well.

- **Bandanna.**
  Can help distinguish him from game in hunting season.

- **Leash.**
  Leather lasts forever but if there's water in your dog's future, consider quick-drying nylon.

- **Water.**
  Carry 8 ounces for every hour of hiking.

I want my dog to help carry water, snacks and other supplies on the trail. Where do I start?

To select an appropriate dog pack measure your dog's girth around the rib cage. A dog pack should fit securely without hindering the dog's ability to walk normally.

Will my dog wear a pack?

Wearing a dog pack is no more obtrusive than wearing a collar, although some dogs will take to a pack easier than others. Introduce the pack by draping a towel over your dog's back in the house and then having your dog wear an empty pack on short walks. Progressively add some crumpled newspaper and then bits of clothing. Fill the pack with treats and reward your dog from the stash. Soon your dog will associate the dog pack with an outdoor adventure and will eagerly look forward to wearing it.

🐾 *How much weight can I put into a dog pack?*

Many dog packs are sold by weight recommendations. A healthy, well-conditioned dog can comfortably carry 25% to 33% of its body weight. Breeds prone to back problems or hip dysplasia should not wear dog packs. Consult your veterinarian before stuffing the pouches with gear.

🐾 *How does a dog wear a pack?*

The pack, typically with cargo pouches on either side, should ride as close to the shoulders as possible without limiting movement. The straps that hold the dog pack in place should be situated where they will not cause chafing.

🐾 *What are good things to put in a dog pack?*

Low density items such as food and poop bags are good choices. Ice cold bottles of water can cool your dog down on hot days. Don't put anything in a dog pack that can break. Dogs will bang the pack on rocks and trees as they wiggle through tight spots in the trail. Dogs also like to lie down in creeks and other wet spots so seal items in plastic bags. A good use for dog packs when on day hikes around the Delaware Valley is trail maintenance - your dog can pack out trash left by inconsiderate visitors before you.

🐾   *Are dog booties a good idea?*

Although not typically necessary, dog booties can be an asset, especially for the occasional canine hiker whose paw pads have not become toughened. Trails can be rocky and in some places there may be broken glass or roots. Hiking boots for dogs are designed to prevent pads from cracking while trotting across rough surfaces.

🐾   *What should a doggie first aid kit include?*

Even when taking short hikes it is a good idea to have some basics available for emergencies:

- 4" square gauze pads
- cling type bandaging tapes
- topical wound disinfectant cream
- tweezers
- insect repellent - no reason to leave your dog unprotected against mosquitoes and biting flies
- veterinarian's phone number

The Other End Of The Leash

Leash laws are like speed limits - everyone seems to have a private interpretation of their validity. Some dog owners never go outside with an unleashed dog; others treat the laws as suggestions or disregard them completely. It is not the purpose of this book to tell dog owners where to go to evade the leash laws or reveal the parks where rangers will look the other way at an unleashed dog. Nor is it the business of this book to preach vigilant adherence to the leash laws. Nothing written in a book is going to change people's behavior with regard to leash laws. So this will be the last time leash laws are mentioned, save occasionally when we point out the parks where dogs are welcomed off leash.

Low Impact Hiking
With Your Dog

Every time you hike with your dog on the trail you are an ambassador for all dog owners. Some people you meet won't believe in your right to take a dog on the trail. Be friendly to all and make the best impression you can by practicing low impact hiking with your dog:

- Pack out everything you pack in.

- Do not leave dog scat on the trail; if you haven't brought plastic bags for poop removal bury it away from the trail and topical water sources.

- Hike only where dogs are allowed.

- Stay on the trail.

- Do not allow your dog to chase wildlife.

- Step off the trail and wait with your dog while horses and other hikers pass.

- Do not allow your dog to bark - people are enjoying the trail for serenity.

- *Have as much fun on your hike as your dog does.*

The Best of the Best

Blue Ribbon - French Creek State Park

Approximately 40 miles of trails visit every corner of French Creek's 7,339 acres. There are nine featured hikes on wide dirt paths of between one and four hours' duration. The marquee walk is the *Boone Trail*, a six-mile loop connecting all the major attractions of the park. Two large lakes make first rate canine swimming holes.

#2 - Andorra Natural Area/Fairmount Park

America's first public park and home of the Philadelphia Art Museum, is the largest contiguous landscaped municipal park in the world, sprawling across nearly 9,000 acres. It is the bucolic home to an estimated 2,500,000 trees and on weekend mornings it can seem as if there is a dog for every one. If the communal dog walking on *Forbidden Drive* isn't for you, take to the hills and try the extensive trail system up the slopes of Wissahickon Gorge.

#3 - Valley Forge National Historic Park

These are some of the most historic walks in America and some of the most beautiful in greater Philadelphia - panoramic vistas from rolling hills, long waterside hikes and climbs up wooded mountainsides. If you're not up to mingling with the tourists, cross the Schuylkill River and try the 3-mile linear *Schuylkill River Trail* that connects the Pawling's Parking Area and the Betzwood Picnic Area. The flat dirt trail hugs the river the entire way. Dogs are welcome throughout the historic park.

#4 - White Clay Creek State Park/Preserve

The Lenni Lenape recognized the great beauty of the White Clay Creek and made their most important "Indian Town" along its banks. There are eight marked trails at White Clay Creek, a state park in Delaware and a state preserve in Pennsylvania. The *Penndel Trail* connects the two as it traces the meanderings of the stream. If you can't get enough of the great hiking with your dog here, two new tracts of land have recently opened nearby under the administration of White Clay Creek State Park.

#5 - Scott Arboretum
Several area colleges welcome responsible dog owners - Swarthmore's Scott Arboretum is the best walk. The collections are integrated with the stone buildings of the college which dates to 1864. Leaving the cultivated plantings of the campus, a variety of hillside trails lead through the 200-acre Crum Woods down to Crum Creek. Dogs are not only welcomed at Swarthmore, but there are water bowls chained to some of the drinking fountains. In the Crum Woods your dog need only be under voice control, not leashed.

#6 - Woodlawn Trustees Property
Adjacent to the popular Brandywine Creek State Park (with 8 trails and 14 miles of hiking of its own) are more than 2,000 acres open to the public for hiking and riding. Miles of informal trails can be combined to create any kind of day out with your dog. Athletic dogs will enjoy romping across the grassy hills above the Brandywine Creek. Walking back and forth on the *Fire Trail* along the water provides an easy 45-minute stroll. The Woodlawn trails serve up as fine a mix of open meadow and mature woodlands hiking as you're likely to find in greater Philadelphia.

#7 - Green Lane Park
Dogs are not allowed on the *Hemlock Point Trail* but there is plenty of rich canine hiking on the park's other four trails to set tails to wagging. The *Red Trail*, designed as an equestrian trail but not chewed up like so many other such surfaces, winds through open fields and stands of trees for 10 miles, although the entire length can be aborted in several places. The premier trail at Green Lane Park is the heavily wooded *Blue Trail* on the western edge of the reservoir where you pick your way across steep ravines and narrow ridges for 6 miles.

#8 - Ridley Creek State Park
The park chains water bowls around its benches along the *Multi-Use Trail* and your dog will welcome the cool drink after tackling the 12 miles of hilly Ridley Creek State Park trails. If the park's four main blazed trails don't tire her out try an unmarked trailhead just east of Ridley Creek on Gradyville Road offers one of the longest creekside walks in Delaware County.

#9 - Monocacy Hill

There are five miles of interesting trail time on Monocacy Hill with the star being the white-blazed Monocacy Hill Trail that scales the 860-foot hilltop that dominates the surrounding landscape. Views extend to the west from the summit. Providing a contrast to the hill climb is the green-blazed *Creek Trail* that scampers through a wet, low-lying area to loop around a small waterfall and pool. Various connecting trails circle around the hill on wide, wooded paths. Hunting is allowed on Monocacy Hill so plan a Sunday trip with your dog in huntng season.

The heights on Monacacy Hill make a great lookout for your trail dog.

#10 - Wharton State Forest

Wharton State Forest lies at the heart of New Jersey's mysterious Pine Barrens, a tapestry of impenetrable scrub pine, swamps and bogs that is the stomping ground of the notorious Jersey Devil. The main pathway is the *Batona Trail*, a 49-mile pink-blazed wilderness trail that begins at Ongs Hat in the north and ends at Lake Absegami in Bass River State Forest to the south. The hard-packed sand trail, that sports some gentle undulations to break up a mostly flat walk, is a joy under paw and boot. The Batsto River flowing through the forest is stained the color of tea by cedar sap, adding to the region's mystique. It makes an excellent canine swimming pool.

No Dogs

Before we get started on the best places to take your dog, let's get out of the way some of the parks that do not allow dogs at all:

NEW JERSEY

Burlington County
Rancocas Nature Center

Camden County
Palmyra Cove Nature Park

Gloucester County
Ceres Park
Greenwich Lake Park
Red Bank Battlefield Park
Scotland Run Park
Washington Lake Park

PENNSYLVANIA

Bucks County
Bowman's Hill Wildflower Preserve
Churchville Nature Center
Five Mile Woods Forest Preserve
Honey Hollow Environmental Education Center
Peace Valley Nature Center

Chester County
Battle of the Clouds Park
Binky Lee Preserve
Crow's Nest Preserve
East Whiteland Township Preserve
Great Valley Nature Center
Jenkins Arboretum
Kardon Park
Kerr Park
Sharp's/Canterbury Woods
Stroud Preserve
Valley Creek Park

Delaware County
Hildacy Farm
Saw Mill Park
The Willows Park
Tyler Arboretum
Wawa Preserve

Montgomery County
Alverthorpe Park
Briar Bush Nature Center
Gwynned Wildlife Preserve
Lorimer County Park
Mill Grove/Audubon Wildlife Sanctuary
Morris Arboretum
Saunders Woods
Stone Hills Wildlife Preserve
Upper Schuylkill Valley Park

O.K. that wasn't as bad as it could be. Let's forget about these and move on to some of the great places where we CAN take our dogs on Philadelphia area trails...

The 50 Best Places To Hike With Your Dog Around Philadelphia...

Pennsylvania

Anson B. Nixon Park

The Park

The land here, featuring a 22-foot drop in the East Branch of the Red Clay Creek, was bought in 1795 by William Chambers to build a mill. He was looking to clean wool. Chambers named his property and fine mansion "Bloom-field," in honor of Brigadier General Bloomfield who drilled 3000 troops on his brother's adjoining property in preparation for the War of 1812. The first organized school in the borough was conducted in a grove of trees here in 1830, a quarter-century before Kennett Square was incorporated. The property remained in the Chambers family for more than a century. The mansion burned and the 82-acre park was established in 1982.

Chester County

Phone Number
- (610) 388-1303

Website
- ken-net.com/kennpark

Admission Fee
- None

Directions
- *Kennett Square*; From Route 1, exit onto State Street and make a right at the bottom of Miller's Hill (the first one heading into town) onto N. Walnut Street. Make a left into the park at the fork 1/4 mile ahead. You can also access the park by taking Route 82 South from Route 1 and make your first left onto Leslie Road, past the Saint Patrick Cemetery. A small parking lot is by the ballfield at the end of the lane.

The Walks

The park is essentially carved into three main segments, each featuring a walking loop. The *Beechwood Trail* in the Beech Woods slips between rare umbrella magnolias and tupelos dressed in gnarly trunks deformed from a bacterial infection. Also here is the signature Kennett Beech which stood when William Penn came from England to claim his land grant more than 300 years ago. The Bloomfield Trail circles two small ponds at the center of the property. The *Otherplace Trail*, named for the home of Cyrus Chambers, penetrates the Pine Woods on the eastern side of the park. Informal spur trails also run through Nixon Park. This is easy walking with only minor dips and rolls along the way on crushed gravel and packed dirt trails.

Bonus
A small remnant of the forests that blanketed southeastern Pennsylvania at the time of 17th century European settlement remain in the park. It retains the species diversity of the original woodland, with a mix of native trees rarely found in this area. The area's biodiversity is described on interpretive signs along the trails.

Trail Sense: The trails are unmarked but the many segments are short and any misdirection will not leave you lost for long. A painted map board is available in a kiosk in the parking lot.

Dog Friendliness
Dogs are welcome along all the trails here.

Traffic
Anson Nixon is a bustling town park with an active recreation area but the wooded trails are less used.

Canine Swimming
The Red Clay Creek is not deep enough for anything beyond splashing. The ponds are set below the level of the trails, providing tricky access at times.

Trail Time
Less than an hour.

It's easy trotting down the Anson B. Nixon paths.

Darlington Trail

The Park

The *Darlington Trail* was developed by Middletown Township, preserving space near the former Darlington Family Dairy Farm.

The Walks

Half of the yellow-blazed *Darlington Trail* hugs the heavily wooded Chester Creek valley and the other half traverses the meadows and fields of the former farmstead. The entire loop is approximately 2 3/4 miles long. The *Cornucopia Trail*, a shorter path blazed in orange, connects with the *Darlington Trail* and circumnavigates a residential area. The *Darlington Trail* also connects with the *Rocky Run Trail*, a scenic linear walk in open woodlands along the Chester Creek. The trails, for the most part, are wide and easy to negotiate.

To do the entire loop will require several steep climbs away from Chester Creek. You can also treat the trail as an out-and-back linear hike along the creekbed that creates an easy walk.

Trail Sense: The trails are well-marked; there is a detailed map posted on the board at the trailhead.

Delaware County

Phone Number
- (610) 565-2700

Website
- middletowntownship.org

Admission Fee
- None

Directions
- *Middletown Township*; A small parking lot for the Darlington Trail is located on Darlington Road, 1/2 mile from Route 1. The parking lot is marked by a trailhead sign.

"A door is what a dog is perpetually on the wrong side of."
-James Thurber

Bonus

In July 1920, Babe Ruth took his big four-door touring sedan on a Yankee roadtrip from Philadelphia to Washington. It was a jolly trip on the way back for Ruth, his wife and three teammates, including stops for bootleg liquor. Singing and driving much too fast past midnight, Ruth failed to negotiate a turn on Route 1 near here and flipped his car. No one was hurt and all walked to a nearby farmhouse to spend the night. Ruth returned the next day with a mechanic to look at the tangled wreckage in the daylight. When he saw it, he said simply, "Sell it." The entourage made their way to Philadelphia, greeted by newspaper headlines screaming, "Ruth Reported Killed In Car Crash."

Dog Friendliness

Dogs are welcome to hike along the *Darlington Trail*.

Traffic

Despite being in the shadow of Route 1, the Darlington Trail is lightly used - the parking lot scarcely holds a half dozen vehicles.

Canine Swimming

At a 270-degree turn in the Chester Creek behind the parking lot, the banks are sandy, giving your dog the opportunity for a rare Delaware County beach experience. Rocky Run, which joins the Chester Creek on the trail is more for splashing.

Trail Time

More than an hour.

Evansburg
State Park

The Park

This land was part of William Penn's American Province purchased from the Lenni Lenape Nation in 1684. The area developed rapidly; by 1714 settlers were sending goods to Philadelphia via the Skippack (from the Lenape word for "wetland") Pike. The agrarian ways of the Mennonites in the Skippack Valley began to evaporate in the years following World War II and plans began for setting aside the land that became Evansburg State Park. The park officially opened for public use on June 28, 1974.

Montgomery County

Phone Number
- (610) 409-1150

Website
- dcnr.state.pa.us/ stateparks/evansburg.htm

Admission Fee
- None

Directions
- *Collegeville*; east of town. From Route 29, pick up Germantown Pike across the Perkiomen Bridge. Make a left on Skippack Creek Road; continue straight onto May Hill Road into the Main Park Area.

The Walks

Although Evansburg comprises more than 3,000 acres, most of the property is set aside for hunting and trapping. There are 6 miles of hiking trails, primarily on the *Skippack Creek Loop Trail* which is essentially two linear trails on either side of the Skippack Creek. This is mostly easy walking with some moderate ups and downs, although the trail on the far side of the Skippack Creek can rise some 100 feet above the water. On the Main Park Area side the trail is wider and flatter, the far side is woodsier and more scenic. Another 15 miles of walking is available on equestrian trails.

Trail Sense: Trails are blazed and a map is available but the Skippack Loop never leaves the creek for more than a few yards.

Bonus
**Germantown Pike was the first road to be started in Montgomery County, dating to 1687 when funds were allocated for a "cart road" from Philadelphia to the Plymouth Meeting settlement. Later extended to present-day Collegeville, an eight arch stone bridge was built to span Skippack Creek in 1792.
An equestrian trail crosses the bridge, which is the oldest bridge in continuous, heavy use in America.**

Dog Friendliness

All trails are open to dogs.

Traffic

Although there are not a wide variety of trails to choose from in Evansburg State Park, the traffic load is not overbearing. You will not, however, find the solitude of other parks here.

Canine Swimming

The Skippack Creek is seldom deep enough for sustained dog-paddling and there are no ponds in the park.

Trail Time

More than an hour.

Skippack Creek makes a splendid canine swimming hole.

"Money will buy a pretty good dog but it won't buy the wag of his tail."
-Josh Billings

Fairmount Park - Andorra Natural Area

The Park

America's first public park began here with 5 acres in 1812. Today, Fairmount Park is the largest contiguous landscaped municipal park in the world with nearly 9,000 acres. It is the bucolic home to an estimated 2,500,000 trees.

The Andorra Natural Area, at the park's northern boundary with Montgomery County, evolved from a 19th century private nursery. Ownership of the property dates to 1840 when Richard Wistar named it "Andorra" from a Moorish word meaning "hills covered with trees." One of those trees - a massive sycamore - grew right through an enclosed porch in the house of the nursery's chief plant propagator. The weakening sycamore was cut down in 1981 but the Tree House survives as the Andorra Visitor Center.

Philadelphia County

Phone Number
- (215) 685-9285

Website
- philaparks.org/wvnatand.htm

Admission Fee
- None

Directions
- *Philadelphia*; Andorra is on Northwestern Avenue between Ridge Avenue and Germantown Avenue (Route 422).

The Walks

The main trail at Andorra is a 20-station Nature Hike. There are also a dozen other named trails that branch off this loop. The *Forbidden Drive* begins its 7-mile journey along the Wissahickon Creek to the Schuylkill River here. So named when it was closed to automobiles in the 1920s, your outing on the Forbidden Drive can be shortened by several bridges across the Wissahickon. A natural dirt trail rolls along the opposite bank to create hiking loops.

The best canine hiking comes on these dirt trails when you leave the paved *Forbidden Drive* and climb out of the gorge. These narrow ribbons of dirt crossing the hillsides are a dog's delight time and again.

Bonus

In 1855, a hotel entrepreneur built a new inn on
Rex Avenue. To draw attention to his hostelry he
constructed an Indian from old barn boards and propped
it up on top of a rock overlooking the Gorge.
In 1902, when the Indian Rock Hotel was long gone
but with the silhouette still there, artist Massey Rhind
was commissioned to make a representation of a
"Delaware Indian, looking west to where his people have
gone." The kneeling warrior has gazed up the Wissahickon
Gorge ever since. A switchback trail leads to the
Indian Statue where you can get close enough to pat
his knee. And take in a breathtaking view.

**Climbing off the Forbidden Drive and up into the
Wissahickon Gorge is sure to put a smile on your dog.**

Trail Sense: The paths are blazed and a map of Andorra is available. Mapboards explain the *Forbidden Drive* trail system.

Dog Friendliness

Dogs are welcome on *Forbidden Drive* in Fairmount Park. Carpenter Woods is a popular spot for dogs to congregate.

Traffic

For those seeking a communal dog walking experience, the bustling Forbidden Drive is the place. Those in search of solitary contemplation can take to the hillside trails of the Wissahickon Gorge, although watch out for mountain bikes.

Canine Swimming

The swimming is excellent in the Wissahickon Creek with many access points.

Trail Time

More than an hour.

French Creek State Park

The Park

A wilderness fort once stood on the small stream flowing through these woods that was garrisoned by the French during the French and Indian War and thus "French Creek." The hillsides here were dotted with charcoal hearths throughout the 1800s, fueling the nascent American iron industry. The furnace was stoked for the last time in 1883.

French Creek State Park was originally developed by the federal government during the Depression as a National Park Service Demonstration Area. Civilian Conservation Corps members, organized by President Franklin Roosevelt, built dams, roads and other recreational trappings. These workers also began restoration of the Hopewell Furnace, today a National Historic Site through which several of the park's trails pass. In 1946, the area was transferred to the Commonwealth of Pennsylvania.

Chester/Berks County

Phone Number
- (610) 582-9680

Website
- dcnr.state.pa.us/stateparks/find-apark/frenchcreek/

Admission Fee
- None

Directions
- *Elverson*; northeast of town. From Route 23, take Route 345 North to the south entrance of the park. From the PennsylvaniaTurnpike the park is 7 miles northeast of the Morgantown Interchange (Exit 22).

The Walks

Approximately 40 miles of trails visit every corner of French Creek's 7,339 acres. There are nine featured hikes of between one and four hours' duration. The marquee walk is the *Boone Trail*, a six-mile loop connecting all the major attractions of the park. The *Mill Creek Trail* is a back-country hike that visits Millers Point, a pile of large boulders where you and your dog can easily scramble to the top.

Bonus

Considered by some as the "Orienteering Capital of North America," French Creek has developed a permanent self-guided course for the practitioners of the art of map and compass. Try it and you can challenge your dog's nose in a wayfinding contest.

All the walks are heavily forested with hardwoods - keep an eye out for the ruins of the area's charcoal-burning past. Repeatedly timbered, there is little understory and the trails are almost universally wide and easy to walk. The park is hilly with the steepest - and rockiest - slopes blanketing the eastern section of French Creek.

Trail Sense. Any park administrator desiring to blaze a trail would do well to visit French Creek State Park. Detailed trail maps are also available.

Dog Friendliness

Dogs are welcome on all the trails and in designated campsites but not in swimming areas.

Traffic

Despite its popularity, the sheer size and number of hikes available conspire to create long stretches of solitude, especially in the rugged eastern end of the park. Horses are restricted to the yellow-blazed *Horse-Shoe Trail* and mountain bikes are banned from many trails, including all trails south of Park Road.

Canine Swimming

There is easy access to two lakes, the 21-acre cold water Scotts Run Lake and the 63-acre Hopewell Lake.

Trail Time

More than an hour.

Green Lane Park

The Park

Public recreation here dates to 1939 with the founding of Upper Perkiomen Valley Park. Upon its wedding to Green Lane Reservoir Park, the largest single open space purchase-easement in Montgomery County history, Green Lane Park, was created. The focal point of the 3100-acre park is the Green Lane Reservoir, home to more than a dozen species of freshwater fish.

The Walks

Four of the five trails here are open to dogs (four-legged friends are not welcome on the *Hemlock Point Trail*). The *Red Trail*, designed as an equestrian trail but not chewed up like so many other such surfaces, winds through open fields and stands of trees for 10 miles, although the entire length can be aborted in several places. The premier trail at Green Lane Park is the heavily wooded *Blue Trail* on the western edge of the reservoir where you pick your way across steep ravines and narrow ridges for 6 miles. Watch for passages over loose rocks. The full loop can be cut off at the Turn Around but you'll miss the extravagant rock carvings of falling water at work. At the Hill Road Office, and overlapping the *Blue Trail*, is the *Whitetail Trail*, a self-guided nature walk.

There are hilly climbs throughout Green Lane Park; the gentlest terrain is found on the *Red Trail*.

Trail Sense: A good trail map is available - and do not let go of it. The trails are blazed, but not always energetically. The *Red Trail* uses ribbons

Montgomery County

Phone Number
- (215) 234-4528

Website
- montcopa.org/parks/greenlane.htm

Admission Fee
- None

Directions
- *Green Lane*; heading north on Route 29 there are several approaches to the trails. For the *Orange Trail*, make a left on Snyder Road, drive through the recreation area to the parking lot on Deep Creek Road. For the *Blue Trail*, make a left on Park Road and a right on Hill Road to the trailhead on the left. The *Red Trail* is just off Route 29 on Knight Road.

On the Red Trail, there is an unexpected walk into a young stand of cedar growing on red dirt and the feeling of Utah desert instantly washes over you.

which are sometimes tied to fallen posts. Among the things NOT to try at Green Lane: following the *Orange Trail* from the parking lot as indicated on the map (it is not marked) and trying the *Red Trail* clockwise (there is a reason the map uses directional arrows).

Dog Friendliness

There is plenty of room to hike with the dog at Green Lane without missing the forbidden *Hemlock Point Trail*.

Traffic

Most of the people who use the recreational areas of this popular park are not even aware of some of the trails in the far reaches of Green Lane. Especially on the *Red Trail* you can count on blocking out long stretches of trail time without seeing a soul.

Canine Swimming

There is excellent access to the reservoir from the *Blue Trail*; less so on the *Red Trail*.

Trail Time

More than an hour.

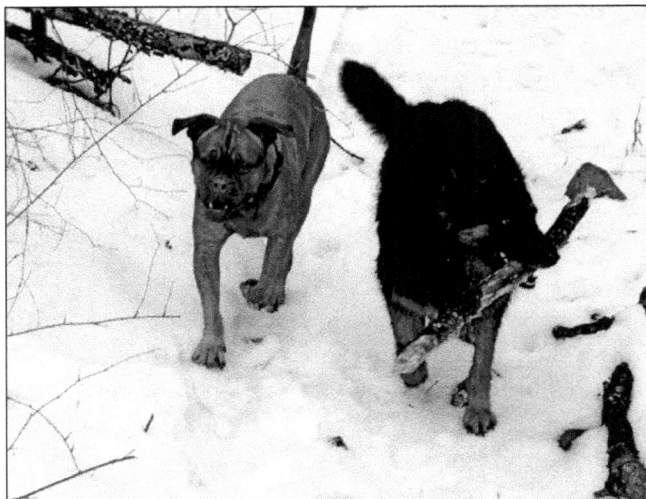

There is great hiking for your dog at Green Lane in any season.

Heinz National Wildlife Refuge

The Park

There are more than 500 National Wildlife Refuges in the United States and only Philadelphia and San Francisco offer an urban environmental study. When the Swedes settled here in 1634, Tinicum Marsh measured over 5,700 acres. Three hundred years later the tidal marsh had been reduced to only 200 acres. The routing of I-95 in 1969 threatened to finish off the marsh but, in ironic fact, saved it. Congress authorized the purchase of 1,200 acres in 1972, establishing the Tinicum National Environmental Center and enabling the highway to roar through the area.

The Walks

You can cover about ten miles of trails here in two major loops. The more attractive of the two is around the Impoundment Marsh near the Visitor Contact Station. If you have a patient dog you can pause at the Observation Platform or one of the Observation Blinds and try to identify one of the 288 species of birds seen in the refuge. The western loop, that begins in Delaware County, leads onto a dike in the middle of the marsh and along the Darby Creek. The trail on the dike is narrow to the point of being overgrown during the spring and summer.

Trail Sense: The trail is not marked nor blazed but there is a map available. It is not detailed and expect to take a detour or two near the Route 420 parking area.

Philadelphia County

Phone Number
- (215) 365-3118

Website
- heinz.fws.gov/

Admission Fee
- None

Directions
- *Philadelphia*; from I-95 take Route 291 for the Philadelphia International Airport. At the first light make a left onto Bartram Avenue. At the third light make a left onto 84th Street. At the second light make a left onto Lindbergh Boulevard. Make a right into the refuge just past the stop sign. The parking area in Delaware County is on Route 420; take Exit 9B off I-95 for Route 420 North. The parking area is right there.

Bonus
There aren't many other places where you can walk
along with your dog and scan the skies alternately for
a Northern Goshawk and a McDonnell-Douglas
or a Buff-Breasted Sandpiper and a Boeing.

Dog Friendliness
Dogs are welcome along all the trails here.

Traffic
There is little competition for space on these trails.

Canine Swimming
The Darby Creek is accessible but the fish pulled from these waters are contaminated so you may want to limit water time here.

Trail Time
More than an hour.

Hibernia County Park

The Park

Property deeds in this area date to October 1, 1765. In the 1790s, Samuel Downing built the first iron forge at Hibernia, along the West Branch of the Brandywine Creek. Downing lost his forge in a sheriff's sale in 1808 and the property then passed rapidly through many owners until Charles Brooke purchased the enterprise in 1821. He expanded its holdings to 1,710 acres and by the Civil War, the Hibernia Iron Works was churning pig iron into bar iron from two forges, two heating furnaces and a rolling mill.

Chester County
Phone Number   - (610) 383-3812
Website   - chesco.org/index.aspx?NID=1743
Admission Fee   - None
Directions   - *Coatesville*; four miles north of town. From Route 30, take Route 82 North two miles to Cedar Knoll Road, turn left and travel 1.25 miles to the main entrance.

The forge went silent in the 1870s. In 1894, Colonel Franklin Swayne, a successful Philadelphia real estate lawyer, purchased the property and transformed Hibernia (the Roman name for Ireland) into a gentleman's country estate. In 1963 the old ironmaster's mansion and nearly 900 acres of surrounding grounds passed to Chester County for renovation as a park.

The Walks

Hibernia features five main trails, all wooded and none longer than 1.5 miles. Only the *Cedar Hollow Trail* loops so you will need to combine park roads and unmarked paths to avoid retracing steps in your walking day. A dirt trail along the Brandywine is one of the longest waterside walks in Chester County.

Most of the walking is easy; there are slight hills down to the Brandywine Creek and the *Rim Trail* across the water requires a good climb to reach the ridge. Mostly the trails are dirt; the *Lake Trail* is paved with crushed stone.

Bonus
A long-time admirer of the English manor tradition, Colonel Swayne made 29 trips to the British countryside to collect ideas for his home. On one such trip he purchased the massive lion heads which adorn the pillar gate posts. It was the colonel who is thought to have covered the stone exterior of the mansion with its distinctive coppery peach stucco.

Trail Sense: The trailheads are marked but some of the trails are more energetically marked than others. Do not let go of the trail map if you attempt to find the _Rim Trail_.

Dog Friendliness
Dogs are welcome along all the trails here.

Traffic
Hibernia is a popular park with facilities for camping and picnicing but it is possible to get away from the crowds, especially across the Brandywine Creek on the _Rim Trail_.

Canine Swimming
Dogs can enjoy a dip in the Brandywine Creek, a fishing pond or in Chambers Lake, where there is limited access to a 90-acre water reservoir created in 1994 with the damming of Birch Run.

Trail Time
More than an hour.

Hibernia County Park serves up some of the Philadelphia area's best creekside hiking along the Brandywine Creek.

Indian Orchard/ Linvill Trails

The Park

In 1986, Middletown Township began preserving significant portions of open space in Middletown in recognition of the Township's Tricentennial. These trails were carved from 157 acres of property acquired from the Linvill family.

The Walks

The *Indian Orchard Trail*, blazed in yellow, rolls through a woodland of mature hardwoods and conifers, crossing five bridges along its one-mile length. The *Linvill Trail* covers 3 1/2 miles over two sections; one, a long perimeter loop around the pasturelands and orchards, the other a fish-hook trail behind Linvilla Orchard. A short spur connects the two trails. These trails are easy hiking, with the *Linvill Trail* the flatter of the two. Indian Orchard features some sporty ups and downs. Take caution on the *Farm Fields Trail* which is sometimes cut from the crop stalks, leaving tiny spears that can injure a pet's paws.

Trail Sense: The trails are marked but are not always distinct when the blazes are on young trees in regenerating woods. The best trail map in Delaware County is available from the township office but not at the trailhead.

Delaware County

Phone Number
- (610) 566-3640

Website
- middletowntownship.org

Admission Fee
- None

Directions
- *Lima*; south of town, just off Route 352 (Middletown Road). The parking lot for the Indian Orchard Trail is at the end of Copes Lane on the western side of Route 352. To reach the Linville Trail from Route 1, make a right on West Knowlton Road and take your first right on Linville Road to the parking lot.

Bonus
**Even into the 20th century indoor plumbing was
not universal and the "necessary" or "outhouse"
was a familiar sight on the rural American landscape.
In the woods along the *Indian Orchard Trail* is a relic
of these times - an abandoned two-seater necessary.**

Dog Friendliness

Dogs are welcome along all the trails here.

Traffic

There is little competition for space on these trails.

Canine Swimming

Crum Run intercepts the *Indian Orchard Trail* several times although it is not deep enough for a full swim. The most water you'll encounter on the *Linville Trail* is at the Hidden Hollow Swim Club, which doesn't welcome dogs in its pools.

Trail Time

More than an hour.

Orchard trees provide welcome shade for hot trail dogs.

Lorimer
Nature Preserve

The Park

The nature preserve, managed by the Open Land Conservancy, is named for George Horimer Lorimer, longtime editor of the *Saturday Evening Post*. Lorimer, a resident of Wyncote, was a pas-sionate conservationist during his lifetime.

The Walks

The Lorimer Preserve is an ideal spot for a walk of less than an hour. The short, interconnecting maze of trails offer a pleasing mix of fields and woods. The walking is easy throughout with many flat streches, especially in the fields. The paths are almost all paw-pleasing grass.

Trail Sense: There are no maps and no blazed trails so your route is left to your imagination. You can criss-cross the property and still find your way back to the parking lot without calling for a St. Bernard-led rescue party.

Dog Friendliness

It sometimes seems as if this park was designed for dog walkers.

Traffic

There are no bikes and no horses allowed on the Lorimer footpaths.

Chester County

Phone Number
- None

Website
- openlandconservancy.org/
George_Lorimer_Nature_Prese.
html

Admission Fee
- None

Directions
- *Tredyffrin Township*; the main entrance is on North Valley Road, north of Swedesford Road. Turn right into the small parking lot up the hill from the bridge across Valley Creek.

The paw-friendly grass trails at Lorimer Preserve will look awfully inviting to your trail dog.

> ### *Bonus*
> **The best stick-fetching pond in greater Philadelphia. Tucked into a hollow in the woods, the pond is scarcely 25 yards across at any point. Your dog can swim across the pond to retrieve a stick and meet you on the other side as you circle the water on land.**

A canine armada enjoys some of the best swimming in the Delaware Valley in the pond at Lorimer Nature Preserve.

Dog Friendliness

It sometimes seems as if this park was designed for dog walkers.

Traffic

There are no bikes and no horses allowed on the Lorimer footpaths.

Canine Swimming

None.

Trail Time

A few minutes to a full day.

Marsh Creek State Park

The Park

To counter frequent flooding in the Brandywine Creek watershed, plans for Marsh Creek Dam began in 1955. Work on the 89-foot earthen dam began in 1970. In 1974 the lake began to fill and six months later 535 acres of what used to be Milford Mills were under up to 73 feet of water. Gone were 42 residences and more than 70 old barns and other structures.

Chester County

Phone Number
- (610) 458-5119

Website
- dcnr.state.pa.us/stateparks/findapark/marshcreek/index.htm

Admission Fee
- None

Directions
- *Upper Uwchlan Township*; the hiking trails at Marsh Creek are reached from Route 282 (Creek Road). From the south, make a right on Reeds Road North. From the north, make a left on Lyndell Road. Both feed into Marsh Creek Road and the parking lot.

The Walks

Marsh Creek Lake dominates the 1,705 acres of the park. There is no hiking at the main entrance on the east side of the lake. All the hiking - six miles worth - lies on the western shores. The main loop (*Bridle Trail*) is interjected with three inner loops. The trail is on a hill overlooking the lake but water views are few. The trails are heavily wooded.

The terrain is hilly leading from the trailhead but easy walking once the high hill is scaled; down the opposite side of the hill the trail hooks into an old railbed along the East Branch of the Brandywine Creek. This stretch of trail, the prettiest in the park, is flat. The trails are mostly dirt although there

Bonus

Theodore Burr built a bridge spanning the Hudson River at Waterford, New York in 1804. He added an arch segment to the multiple truss bridge popular at the time, attaining a longer span. Patented in 1817, the Burr Arch Truss became one of the most common in the construction of covered bridges. The Larkin's Bridge, a 65-foot long, 45-ton "Burr Arch" covered bridge erected in 1854 and rebuilt in 1881, was relocated to the northeast section of the park in 1972. Larkin's Covered Bridge is the only remaining legacy of Milford Mills.

are long patches of rocky ground on the slopes that are tough on foot and paw.

Trail Sense: There are many more trails at Marsh Creek State Park than are indicated on the trail map. An occasional sign pops up to inspire confidence and some blazes but mostly you and the dog are on your own.

Dog Friendliness
Dogs are welcome along the hiking trails here.
Traffic
Marsh Creek is a heavily used park for all manner of recreation. Don't expect to have these trails to yourself.
Canine Swimming
Accessed from the parking lot, Marsh Creek Lake offers the best lake swimming in Chester County; the Brandywine Creek here is usually too shallow for anything more than splashing.
Trail Time
More than an hour.

A prize retrieved from Marsh Creek Lake.

McKaig Nature Education Center

The Park

The Upper Merion Park and Historic Foundation was created in 1964 to preserve the area's rapidly diminishing open space. Small accruals of land gifts began accumulating and today the McKaig Nature Education Center pushes back the encroaching development with 89 wooded acres.

The Walks

A jewel among the region's small parks, McKaig features three wide and well-maintained trails that range in walking time from 15 minutes to 45 minutes. The *Cadet Trail* is a linear exploration running up the spine of the property. Two loop trails branch off the Cadet: the *Nancy Long Trail* and the short, but steep *Laurel Trail*. The loops are hillier than the Cadet Trail but the trails work around the hillside rather than straight up the slopes on these sporty walks.

Trail Sense: The *Cadet Trail* (white blazes) and the *Nancy Long Trail* (yellow blazes) are well-marked. The *Laurel Trail* is unmarked; look for the entrance under a fallen tree.

Buncombe County

Phone Number
- (484) 580-9474

Website
- www.enjoymckaig.org

Admission Fee
- None

Directions
- *Wayne*; bounded roughly by King of Prussia Road, Brower Road and Croton Road. Parking is available on Brower Road (one or two cars on the roadside) and at the Roberts School on Croton Road. From Route 202, take Warner Road south to the end. Make a left on Croton Road and the school is on the right.

*"If there are no dogs in Heaven,
then when I die I want to go where they went."
-Anonymous*

Bonus
This is one of the best places to walk for arboreal education. Many of the trees along the *Nancy Long Trail* are marked for identification, including a rare American Chestnut. The greatest tree in the Colonial forest, the American Chestnut was struck down by a pandemic chestnut blight in the 1930s. Full-grown specimens of the tree have become nearly extinct, although some hardy shoots have survived. But as they mature, they too will fall victim to the fatal blight, as will this sapling.

Dog Friendliness

Dogs are welcome on the trails in the McKaig Nature Education Center.

Traffic

Expect your visit to be a solitary experience.

Canine Swimming

The Crow Creek is a tumbling, pleasing little brook but seldom deep enough for anything beyond doggie splashing.

Trail Time

Up to an hour possible to tackle all the sporty trails here.

The centrally located Crow Creek provides an ideal refresher for your dog after coming down from the wooded slopes of McKaig Nature Center.

Monocacy Hill

The Park

Monocacy Hill Recreation Area is a 420-acre forest located in Amity Township. This recreation area was purchased by Amity Township in 1967 for open space and recreation purposes. The park has a wide variety of plant life. To date, 170 species of herbaceous plants have been identified, along with 65 species of trees and shrubs, and 17 species of ferns and related plants.

The Walks

There are five miles of sporty trail time in store on Monocacy Hill with the star being the white-blazed *Monocacy Hill Trail* that scales the 860-foot hilltop that dominates the surrounding landscape. Views extend to the west from the summit. Providing a contrast to the hill climb is the green-blazed *Creek Trail* that scampers through a wet, low-lying area to loop around a small waterfall and pool. Various connecting trails circle around the hill on wide, wooded paths. Hunting is allowed on Monocacy Hill so plan a Sunday trip with your dog in hunting season.

Trail Sense: Dirt trails and rock-hopping at the summit of the Monocacy Hill monadnock but nothing your dog can't handle. Signposts mark the trail junctions and a map is available.

Berks County

Phone Number
- (800) 354-8383

Website
- monocacyhill.org/

Admission Fee
- None

Directions
- *Douglassville*; take 422 West approximately one mile past Route 662 to right turn at Monocacy Creek Road. Turn right and continue to first stop sign at Loyalsock Drive. Follow to end and turn right on to Hill Road. Follow for .7 mile to Y in road. Bear left at Y on to Geiger Road. Proceed up hill to parking lot on left.

Bonus
The Reading Railroad, once the largest corporation in the world, ran tracks across the southern tier of the property a century ago. Souvenirs of that time include an easy-trotting railbed trail and a unique variety of trackside structures still standing.

Dog Friendliness

Dogs are allowed to hike the trails on Monocacy Hill.

Traffic

Foot traffic only and typically not much of it.

Canine Swimming

The creeks in the conservation area are narrow and shallow

Trail Time

One to two hours.

The steady climb to the lookout on Monocacy Hill is certain to set your dog's tongue to panting.

Neshaminy State Park

The Park

Neshaminy State Park takes its name from the confluence of Neshaminy Creek with the Delaware River. Although the water flows another 116 miles to the Atlantic Ocean, the river is still affected by the tides here. Indian tribes congregated here to build fishing weirs, small fences in the water that fish swim over at high tide and become trapped at low tide. Dunken Williams operated a ferry crossing of the Delaware River at this point in 1679 and Dunks Ferry Road on the eastern boundary of the park has been used for more than 300 years. The land was deeded to the Commonwealth of Pennsylvania in 1956.

Bucks County

Phone Number
- (828) 259-5800

Website
- dcnr.state.pa.us/stateparks/findapark/neshaminy

Admission Fee
- None

Directions
- *Bensalem*; from the Route 132 (Street Road) exit of I-95 go east to State Road. Go left and the park is at the intersection of Dunks Ferry Road, less than one mile away.

The Walks

Neshaminy State Park is the best park in the area to experience the Delaware River. There are four miles of formal hiking trails on the 330-acre property shaped like a fingernail poking into the river. The *River View Trail* traces the shoreline providing access to the tidal marsh and river and affording riveting views of the ship traffic in the Delaware and the Philadelphia skyline. The *River Trail Inner Loop* explores the interior of the park. The *River Walk* is a shaded dirt trail; the inner loop is more open and follows a gravel road. There is an ample grass shoulder that that will save paws. Also available is the *Logan Walk*, a paved, tree-lined path that was the original is the *Logan Walk*, a paved, tree-lined path that was the original drive to the former Robert Logan Home, whose Sarobia estate was the foundation for the park.

Bonus

In the northeast area of the park, along the Neshaminy Creek, are several acres of sand dunes that would not be out of place at the Atlantic seashore. This giant sandbox for your dog is at the end of the *Logan Walk*. Nearby is the Pine Plantation wherewide, grassy swaths of trails wind among tall, fragrant pines.

Trail Sense: The trails are not blazed but a park map is available.

Dog Friendliness

Dogs are welcome along all the trails here but not permitted near the swimming pools at the center of the park.

Traffic

This is a busy park and moments of solitude will be found in bits and pieces and not large chunks.

Canine Swimming

There is some of the best canine swimming in the area at Neshaminy State Park with about a quarter-mile of open access to the Delaware River.

Trail Time

More than an hour.

Testing the sandy patches on the pine plantation that once covered today's Neshaminy State Park.

Norristown Farm Park

The Park

The area that is today Norristown Farm Park was part of a 7000-acre tract of land belonging to William Penn, known as "William-stadt." The ownership of the Norris family dates to October 10, 1704 when Penn's son sold the land to Isaac Norris and William Trent for the hefty sum of 850 pounds. On November 11, 1717, Trent sold his share of the manor to Norris.

After many subsequent lords, in 1876 the Pennsylvania legislature authorized the purchase of the manor for the Norristown State Hospital. The hospital eventually spread across 981 acres, 831 of which became a farm supplying not only food but a supposed conduit to patient recovery. Farm operations became too costly and ceased in 1975 and the farm fell into disrepair. In 1992, Montgomery County leased 690 acres to create the county's second largest park.

Montgomery County

Phone Number
- (610) 270-0215

Website
- dcnr.state.pa.us/stateparks/norris.htm

Admission Fee
- None

Directions
- *Norristown*; the main entrance is off Germantown Pike on Upper Farm Road (the first house on the right along the entrance road is Shannon Mansion, built in 1764 and the oldest building on the property). There is also parking on Whitehall Road.

The Walks

There are wide, multi-use trails totalling more than five miles at Norristown Farm Park. The trails roughly combine to form adjacent loops in a figure-eight pattern, passing through natural areas and cultivated fields of the revitalized farm where corn, soybeans and winter grains grow. The walking is easy across these rolling hills but there are long periods without shade for the heat-sensitive dog. All the trails are paved in macadam.

Bonus
While many of the Hospital Farm's buildings have disappeared, the unique dairy barn remains. Built in 1914, it is shaped like a wheel with four spokes. The fame of the hospital's dairy operation was widespread. In 1961 alone, nine cows produced 1.1 million pounds of milk - more than 300 pounds of milk per cow per day.

Trail Sense: A detailed trail map is available at the Milk House Visitor Center and is posted on boards in the parking lot.

Dog Friendliness
Dogs are welcome along all the trails in Norristown Farm Park.

Traffic
The paved trails are popular with cyclists, roller skaters and joggers. Your dog will need to be kept on a tight rein most of the time here.

Canine Swimming
Two branches of the Stony Creek knife through the property before joining at the baseball field into one stream. Although it reaches a swimming-friendly depth of four feet in places, the water is only accessed by the trail a few times.

Trail Time
About an hour.

All dogs enjoy a day on the farm.

Nottingham
County Park

The Park

Although this area had already been settled for nearly two centuries, it was not until 1828 that serpentinite was dicovered in what is now Nottingham Park. By 1880 the Wood Mine dug to extract the mineral was 800 feet deep and the largest in the world. Chrome, asbestos and quartz were also mined here. Chester County got into the park business with Nottingham, dedicated in 1963. The 651 acre-park rests atop a natural outcropping of serpentine stone more than one square mile wide and you can still see traces of the quarry and mining operations on your visit.

Chester County

Phone Number
- (610) 932-2589

Website
- chesco.org/index.aspx?NID=1744

Admission Fee
- None

Directions
- *Nottingham*; just north of the Pennsylvania-Maryland state line. Take Route 1 South and exit on Route 272, crossing back over the highway to the entrance of Herr's Snack Foods on the right. Make a right when you can turn left to the Herr's Factory and another right (Park Road) to the parking lot on the left.

> **Bonus**
> Nottingham Park is home to the Serpentine Barrens,
> a seven-mile ridge of igneous rock that is one of only
> three such serpentine formations in North America.
> The early settlers called the area of scrub pine and oak
> "barrens" because its low nutrient-level was
> unfriendly to cultivation. The distinctive green serpentine
> rock was a popular building stone and can be seen in many
> of Chester County's historic structures, including several
> at West Chester University. An interpretive nature trail
> describes the fast-draining Serpentine Barrens
> and visits abandoned quarries.

The Walks

There are 8 trails in Nottingham Park, which can all be covered in a day's hiking. Most of the trails criss-cross and do not loop, often just running out at the boundaries of the 600-acre park. Look for the "Mystery Hole," an abandoned mine now filled with water. The dirt trails are generally wide through the rolling hills across the park. These hills can be formidable at times.

Trail Sense: The trails are blazed and named but study the available maps closely so you don't follow a trail to a dead-end at the back of the park without creating a loop. You will often be confronted with signposts at trail junctions. Choose wisely.

The pine scrub trails at Nottingham County Park are unlike any your dog will find in southeast Pennsylvania.

Dog Friendliness

Dogs are welcome along all the trails here.

Traffic

Tucked away in a remote corner of Chester County, the park does not get much visitation on the trails.

Canine Swimming

McPherson Lake and Little Pond are open-field swimming holes for a doggie dip.

Trail Time

More than an hour.

Nockamixon
State Park

The Park

Once a prominent settlement for the Lenni Lenape Indians, Nockamixon State Park was planned and developed by the U.S. Army Corps of Engineers with the damming of the Tohickon Creek. The park officially opened in 1973 and the resulting Lake Nockamixon has become the premier destination for boating in southeast Pennsylvania. Combined with the adjacent State Game Land #157, more than 7,000 acres - the largest open space in Bucks County - is available for public recreation.

The Walks

The Indians called the land "no-cha-miska-ing" - "at the place of soft soil." Little has changed in the 400 years since. These low, often water-level trails are indeed soft and, many

Bucks County

Phone Number
- (215) 529-7300

Website
- dcnr.state.pa.us/stateparks/find-apark/nockamixon

Admission Fee
- None

Directions
- *Quakertown*; Lake Nockamixon is in northcentral Bucks County. The main entrance to the park is located on Route 563 and is reached from the south on Route 413/412. To reach Haycock Mountain in State Game Lands #157 go west 1.1 miles on Route 563 from the junction with Route 412. Turn onto Top Rock Road and go .6 miles to the parking lot on the left.

times, downright squishy. There are more than 20 miles of the soft equestrian trails and a paved 2.8-mile bicycle trail skirts the shoreline as well. A 21-mile circumnavigation of Lake Nockamixon can be parsed together with bridle paths, trails and back roads.

A unique experience awaits the athletic dog at Haycock Mountain in State Game Land #157. The mountain is essentially a ridge of diabase boulders and the trail to the top calls for almost continuous rock-hopping, a technique called bouldering. The basaltic rock provides incredible traction for boot and paw. A narrow, red-blazed and stone-strewn trail leads uphill

Bonus
**At 960 feet Haycock Mountain wants only ten feet
for being the highest point in Bucks County.
Views from the heavily wooded summit are obscured
in the summer but whn the leaves drop a commanding
view of Lake Nockamixon is revealed.**

from the parking lot to the boulder field. After that the trails are marked by white and blue blazes but the way to the top is frequently obfuscated by scores of fallen trees. This bouldering is a walk unlike any other in the region.

Trail Sense: A park map is available to provide a sketchy view of where you are rather than detailed routes; take not that some of the routes do not loop back to the trailhead.

**Your dog will find rocks are a big part
of his hiking day in corners of
Nockamixon State Park.**

Dog Friendliness
Dogs are welcome in the park; approximately 3,000 acres are open to dog training from Labor Day to March 31.

Traffic
Mountain bikers get their own trails and so do horse people - there are more than 35 miles of pathways through the park. Outside the recreational area, there is little trail competition at Nockamixon.

Canine Swimming
The trails seldom touch the densely wooded shores of Lake Nockamixon but there is good swimming when the chance comes.

Trail Time
Anything from a short jaunt to an all-day outing are on the hiking menu for your dog.

"Properly trained, a man can be dog's best friend."
-Corey Ford

Oakbourne Park

The Park

John Hulme built the first granite shelter on this land, selecting the highest area on the property for his home-site. In 1882 a wealthy Philadelphia lawyer named James Smith purchased 143 acres of land on the west side of South Concord Road, including the old Hulme house. Smith renamed it "Oakbourne" and set more than 150 skilled craftsmen to work refurbishing his new summer home. Oakbourne was soon the centerpiece of a 27-acre estate with fountains, miniature lakes and rustic bridges. Smith even had its own private railroad station and post office.

Oakbourne was willed out of the Smith family to the Philadelphia Protestant Episcopal City Mission in 1896 for the operation of a convalescent home for women over 21 years of age. The next 70 years saw thousands of female "guests" treated here before the costly operation overwhelmed its directors. Westtown Township saved Oakbourne from developers in 1974, eventually creating a 90-acre park.

Chester County

Phone Number
- None

Website
- None

Admission Fee
- None

Directions
- *Westtown*; coming south on Route 202, make a left on Matlack Street (the first traffic light at the end of the highway), which runs into Oakbourne Road and South Concord Road. Make a right into the driveway and proceed past the mansion to the parking lot. Coming north on Route 202, make a right on Route 926 (Street Road) and a left on Concord Road. The park is on the left.

The Walks

Three connecting trails (*Creek*, *Nature* and *Park*) form a loop of nearly three miles to visit all areas of the park on both sides of Concord Road. The trails are all wooded, including native specimens and the remains of the Smiths' exotic plantings around the Victorian stone mansion. There is an interesting mix of terrain and sights on the remains of the country estate

Bonus
The most striking feature of the country estate was a 1,000-gallon, twin-tank water tower built on the lawn away from the mansion. Built of stone and brick to resemble a fortress, the tower features dormer-style twin roofs. Smith installed the finest of telescopes at Oakbourne that offered views across the countryside to the towns of Chester and Philadelphia.

now engulfed by residential development. There are some dips and rolls in some of the wooded areas, including one good climb on the *Creek Trail*.

Trail Sense: The trails are haphazardly marked in places (the blazes are the smallest in Chester County) and can be hard to follow, especially picking the trail up across Concord Road. A mapboard is available near the parking lot.

Dog Friendliness
Dogs are welcome along all the trails here.

Traffic
The lightly tapped trails at Oakbourne are shoehorned into a tight geographic area that doesn't afford much isolation.

Canine Swimming
Part of the trail hopscotches past Chester Creek and one of Smith's miniature lakes, encircled by reeds, is a pleasant canine swimming stop.

Trail Time
At least an hour is possible.

"And sometimes when you'd get up in the middle of the night you'd hear the reassuring thump, thump of her tail on the floor, letting you know that she was there and thinking of you."
                                                            -William Cole

Pennypack Park

The Park

Pennypack Park gets its name from the Lenni-Lenape Indians who hunted and fished along the creek for hundreds of years. The name means "dead deep water." Pennypack Park has often been called the Cradle of American Ornithology due to work done here by John James Audubon and Alex- ander Wilson. The City of Philadelphia established the park in 1905 to insure protection of 1600 acres of woodlands and wetlands.

Philadelphia County

Phone Number
- (828) 877-3265

Website
- pennypackpark.org

Admission Fee
- None

Directions
- *Northeast Philadelphia*; Pennypack Park stretches from the eastern border of Montgomery County almost to the Delaware River. Parking is generally available near the major north-south cross roads through the park.

The Walks

Pennypack Park is the younger, rougher brother to the Wissahickon Gorge and Fairmount Park. The adventurous canine hiker can search out miles of little-used side trails, many quite narrow, off the main 18-mile multi-use trail. The land around the Pennypack Creek is modestly hilly, although you can walk for a long time without noticing it. The multi-use trail is paved. Watch for paw-slicing glass on some of the dirt trails.

Trail Sense: Pennypack Park is for the canine explorer; there are no maps or trail blazes or mapboards, save for the general route of the multi-use trail. Let your dog lead the way.

"Children are for people who can't have dogs."
-Anonymous

Bonus

The fall line on the Pennypack Creek was the natural choice for fording the creek back to Indian days. William Penn was not so patient in waiting for the tide to take the water away each day and in 1683 he asked that "an order be given for building a bridge over the Pennypack." Each male resident was taxed in either money or labor to build the bridge, that, when completed in 1697, became the first Three Arch Stone bridge in America. Designated a National Civil Engineering Landmark, the bridge over Frankford Avenue in Pennypack Park is the oldest stone bridge still carrying heavy traffic in America.

Dog Friendliness

Dogs are welcome in Pennypack Park.

Traffic

Pennypack is a busy city park with a few side excursions available for solitude seekers.

Canine Swimming

The fall line of the Pennypack Creek is in the park south of Frankford Avenue where the last set of rapids play out and the water drops to the level of its final destination, the Delaware River. After the fall line, the tides change the swimming pools from shallow to deep and back again in a twice-repeated daily cycle.

Trail Time

More than an hour.

Taking advantage of the cool flowing waters in Pennypack Creek.

Pennypack Preserve

The Park

The privately owned Pennypack Ecological Restoration Trust has been assembling a natural area preserve since 1970. Using land purchases, donations and conservation easements, the preserve has grown to 683 acres.

The Walks

There are 7 miles of trails here; dogs are allowed only in the Wilderness Area. Three connecting trails, each with its own personality, create a linear trail along the Pennypack Creek for about 2 1/2 miles. The longest, the *Deep Creek Road Trail*, is a country lane walk with plenty of access to the meandering stream. The middle leg, the *Pennypack Creek Trail*, hugs a hillside and is characterized by tall trees, especially conifers. The Pennypack Parkway is an old gravel access road, draped in a shaded canopy of trees. The walking here is mostly level with imperceptible ups and downs along the way.

Trail Sense: There are signposts and a trail map is available at the trailhead. Do not take any of the spur trails as they lead into the Environmental Management Center where dogs are not allowed.

Montgomery County

Phone Number
- (215) 657-0830

Website
- liberty.net.org/pert/mission.htm

Admission Fee
- None

Directions
- *Bryn Athyn*; on western edge of town. The trailhead for the wilderness trails is at the corner of Terwood Road and Creek Road. From the intersection of Huntingdon Pike (Route 232) and Old Welsh Road (Route 63), go west on Old Welsh Road and make the first right across the bridge onto Terwood Road. Creek Road is one mile on the right. The trails can also be accessed from Mason's Mill Park on Mason's Mill Road.

Bonus
A floodplain is a safety valve for the release of a raging creek's overflow. Along the *Paper Mill Trail*, just off the *Creek Road Trail*, is an exhibit on managing these protective wetlands that create a unique wildlife habitat. The stone double-arch bridge next to the floodplain exhibit was built in 1847.

Dog Friendliness
Although dogs are confined to the ribbon of trail along the Pennypack Creek, it is best remembered that most private nature preserves don't allow them at all.

Traffic
A long linear trail that requires a hiker's commitment, there is not as much traffic as the quality of the walk might otherwise inspire. There is some bicycle traffic to dodge.

Canine Swimming
The Pennypack Creek is seldom more than two feet deep, save for the base of Huntingdon Road where there are deep pools for doggie paddling.

Trail Time
More than an hour.

How To Pet A Dog
Tickling tummies slowly and gently works wonders.
Never use a rubbing motion; this makes dogs bad-tempered.
A gentle tickle with the tips of the fingers is all that is necessary to induce calm in a dog. I hate strangers who go up to dogs with their hands held to the dog's nose, usually palm towards themselves.
How does the dog know that the hand doesn't hold something horrid?
The palm should always be shown to the dog and go straight down to between the dog's front legs and tickle gently with a soothing voice to acompany the action. Very often the dog raises its back leg in a scratching movement, it gets so much pleasure from this.
-Barbara Woodhouse

Ralph Stover/ Tohickon Valley Park

The Park

Ralph Stover State Park takes its name from the operator of a water-powered grain mill on the Tohickon Valley Creek in the late 1700s. Traces of the historic mill can still be seen above the dam. The Stover descendants donated the property to Pennsylvania in 1931 and recreational facilities in the 45-acre park were constructed during the 1930s by the Works Project Administration The High Rocks area was donated by celebrated Bucks County author James Michener.

Bucks County

Phone Number
- (610) 982-5560

Website
- dcnr.state.pa.us/stateparks/findapark/ralphstover

Admission Fee
- None

Directions
- *Point Pleasant*; two miles north of town on State Park Road and Stump Road. Tohickon Valley Park is two miles down Cafferty Road off Route 32.

The Walks

The *Red Dot Trail* sweeps in a wide arc for 5.5 miles connecting the two parks. Upon reaching the top of the High Rocks it is easy to feel like you have been parachuted into the heart of the Applachian mountains. Two hundred feet below you stretches a hillside tapestry of trees collared by a horsehoe turn in the Tohickon Creek. There is no similar view in the Delaware Valley. The trail itself rolls up and down across several ravine-slashing creeks. The dirt path is wide and easy on the paws, save for a steady diet of hopping on and across exposed tree roots.

Three short walking trails course through Ralph Stover State Park and additional trails are maintained in Tohickon Valley Park across the creek for extended canine hiking.

Trail Sense: The "Red Dot" trail is well-blazed and a trail map is available.

Bonus
**The chance to watch experienced rock climbers
tackling the 200-foot sheer rock face of the
Tohickon Palisades. Climbers have identified
more than three dozen routes up the slate-like rock.**

Dog Friendliness

Dogs are welcome in the park.

Traffic

The "Red Dot" trail is popular with mountain bikers; foot traffic thins considerably away from the High Rocks vista.

Canine Swimming

The fast-flowing waters of the Tohickon can be treacherous when the water is high.

Trail Time

At least an hour to a half-day.

**The High Rocks along the Tohickon Creek serve up views
your dog won't see anywhere else in the Delaware Valley.**

"The best thing about a man is his dog."
-French Proverb

Ridley Creek State Park

The Park

Settlement in this area dates back to the 1600s when villages grew around the mills sprinkled along the creeks and streams. Much of the park's 2,606 acres were consolidated in the Jefford family - their Hunting Hill mansion, built in 1914 around a 1789 stone farmhouse, now serves as the park office. The Commonwealth of Pennsylvania purchased the property in the 1960s - including 35 historic residences - and the park was dedicated in 1972.

The Walks

Ridley Creek features 12 miles of hiking on four main trails. The *White Trail* visits most of the areas of the park and the others intersect this lengthy loop at many points. A 5-mile multi-use loop is shared with bicyclists and joggers. Also, an unmarked trailhead just east of Ridley Creek on Gradyville Road offers one of the longest creekside walks in Delaware County. In addition, a 4.7-mile equestrian trail makes two large loops in the isolated western section of the park.

These heavily wooded trails are narrow in many places and you and the dog will be prime targets for hitchhiking ticks. Most of the trails wind through rolling woodland and meadows. You'll be moving up and down often but only an occasional hardy climb is necessary.

Trail Sense: The trails are blazed and easy to follow, except through the parking areas - keep your eye on the pavement here. A trail map is available.

Delaware County

Phone Number
- (610) 892-3900

Website
- dcnr.state.pa.us/stateparks/findapark/ridleycreek

Admission Fee
- None

Directions
- *Newtown Square*; Ridley Creek can be accessed from Route 3, 2.5 miles west of Newtown Square, past the Colonial Pennsylvania Plantation. The park may also be entered from Gradyville Road - east from Route 352 or west from Route 252.

Bonus

A handful of historic 18th century structures stand intact within park boundaries and are leased as highly coveted private residences. A group of these stone buildings include a miller's house, office and library, and several small millworkers' houses that have been designated as the "Ridley Creek Historic District" on the National Register of Historic Places.

Dog Friendliness

Dogs are welcome on all the trails; along the multi-use trail are metal doggie water bowls chained to the benches.

Traffic

If you opt off the *Multi-Use Trail* you can go miles in Ridley Creek without seeing other hikers and dogs. Bikes are not allowed off the paved trails.

Canine Swimming

Ridley Creek, while extremely scenic, is only deep enough for canine aquatics in spots. There are no ponds on the property.

Trail Time

Up to a half-day of hiking with your dog here.

With trails on both sides of Ridley Creek your dog is seldom far from a quick dip.

Riverbend Education Center

The Park

The Riverbend story begins 300,000,000 years ago when a crack in the rock known as the Rosemont Fault turned what would become known as the Schuylkill River a full 90 degrees. The first settlers came to the area in the 1500s when the Lenni-Lenape Indians began planting vegetables in an area known as "Indian Fields." In 1904, Howard Wood, brother of steel magnate Alan Wood, created a 52-acre farm inside the river's elbow. Three generations later, in 1974, his descendents deeded half of the farm to serve as a wildlife refuge known as Riverbend Environmental Education Center.

Montgomery County

Phone Number
- (610) 527-5234

Website
- gladwyne.com/riverbend/

Admission Fee
- None

Directions
- *Gladwyne*; from the Blue Route (I-476) North, take Exit 6A for Conshohocken, Route 23 East. Make a left on Spring Mill Road, continue past the Philadelphia Country Club and bear left at the end of the road to the Education Center parking lot.

The Walks

The feature trail at Riverbend, amidst two miles of hiking, is the *Aloha Trail* that circles the perimeter of the property. Unfortunately the walk is marred by the relentless pounding of traffic on the Schuylkill Expressway below. Look for Fiveleaf Akebia, an invasive plant that covers everything on the hillside above the roadway. The other trails are short connecting spurs of only several minutes duration. Avoid the Jack-in-the-Pulpit and Poplar trails - they can be overgrown. Another hike here is *Sid Thayer's Trail*, a linear trail on private property that is also plagued by traffic noise. Riverbend is situated on the knob of a hill and there is little flat walking to be had here.

Trail Sense: There is a hand-painted mapboard at the parking lot for orientation. On the trails there are signposts at junctions. The *Aloha Trail* is

Bonus
**The Visitor Center is a restoration of a 1923
Sears & Roebuck mail order barn. A century ago
Sears sold anything and everything by mail -
including kits for building houses and barns.
The kit, which could cost as little as a few hundred
dollars depending on style, would include rough lumber,
framing timbers, plank flooring, shingles, hardware,
sash and paint. Usually shipped by train from the west,
the barn kit would be loaded onto a freight wagon
and hauled to the building site for assembly by
local carpenters.**

blazed in red and marked by trail signs which are handy through the tricky residential passage.

Dog Friendliness
Dogs are welcome along all the trails here.
Traffic
Aside from school groups during the week there is little competition on the trails at Riverbend.
Canine Swimming
Riverbend sports the smallest pond in the tri-state area, alongside the *Bluebird Trail*. Although scarcely ten feet across, smaller dogs can motor around and larger ones can drop in to cool off.
Trail Time
About an hour.

**Invasive plants in the understory
blanket the trails at Riverbend
Education Center.**

Schuylkill Canal Park

The Park

Pennsylvania's first canal system was cobbled together in 1815 using 120 locks to stretch 108 miles from the coal fields of Schuylkill County to Philadelphia. Railroads began chewing away at canal business in the 1860s and the last coal barges floated down the Schuylkill River in the 1920s. Today, the only sections of the canal in existence are at Manayunk and Lock 60, built by area name donor Thomas Oakes, at the Schuylkill Canal Park. In 1985 the Schuylkill Canal Association formed to keep the canal flowing and maintain the lock and towpath. In 1988, the area was added to the National Register of Historic Places.

Montgomery County

Phone Number
- (610) 917-0021

Website
- schuylkillcanal.org

Admission Fee
- None

Directions
- *Mont Clare*; on Route 29 across the Schuylkill River from Phoenixville. Crossing the river on Bridge Street, make a left at the end of the bridge onto the entrance road for the upstream parking area. To reach the downstream parking lot make the right at the light onto Port Providence Road and follow it through town and past the Container Corporation of America.

The Walks

You can either enjoy the flattest walk in Montgomery County here or the steepest. The peaceful canal towpath covers 2 1/2 miles from the Lock House, built in 1836, to the eastern end of Port Providence. Across the canal are houses and town buildings looking much as they did throughout the canal era.

Upstream from Lock 60 are the *Ravine Trail*, with three ascents to the 100-foot high rock bluffs overlooking the Schuylkill River, and the *Valley View Trail*, which deadends - for dogwalking - at the Upper Schuylkill Valley Park. No dogs are allowed in that park. There is also an eight-station self-guided nature walk from the Lock House to Route 29.

Trail Sense: Just follow the canal.

Bonus
**Upstream from Black Rock Dam is a rocky crag
that towers 100 feet over the water and carries the
following 19th century lore: "A stunted cedar grew
upon the very verge and it made the most masculine heart
tremble to stand upon the edge and while clinging to this
frail support look down into the waters beneath.
Sometime after the settlement when the natives
had been in contact with the whites long enough to
acquire their vices an Indian was tempted with the
promise of a bottle of whiskey to leap three times
from this crag into the river. Twice he made the
terrible plunge successfully. Returning after the
second attempt wearied with the unwanted exertion
and bleeding from wounds made by some sharp
stones against which he had struck he sprang
again into the stream never more to appear."
Since that time it has borne the name of Indian Rock.**

Dog Friendliness

This is one of the friendliest, most relaxed parks in the area.

Traffic

Very light; your primary worry being the entrance road which is only 1 1/2 cars wide.

Canine Swimming

Virtually every step of the way there is great access to either the Schuylkill River or the Schuylkill Canal.

Trail Time

More than an hour.

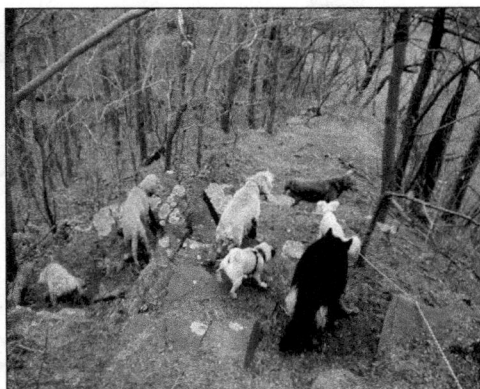

**The trails climb steeply above the Schuylkill
River at the Schuylkill Canal Park.**

Scott Arboretum

The Park

The 300-acre Swarthmore campus is developed to be an arboretum, established in 1929 as a living memorial to Arthur Hoyt Scott, Class of 1895. The 3,000 different kinds of plants have been chosen as suggestions for the best trees, shrubs, perennials and annuals to use in home gardens in the Delaware Valley.

The Walks

Several area colleges welcome responsible dog owners - Swarthmore's Scott Arboretum serves the best canine hiking. The plant collections are integrated with the stone buildings of the college that dates to 1864. Leaving the cultivated plantings of the campus, a variety of hillside trails lead through the 200-acre Crum Woods down to Crum Creek.

Trail Sense: Brochures and mapboards lead you around these delightful walks.

Delaware County

Phone Number
- (610) 328-8025

Website
- scottarboretum.org

Admission Fee
- None

Directions
- *Swarthmore*; on Chester Road (Route 320) between I-95 and Baltimore Pike. Parking for the arboretum is just inside the entrance on College Road, on the left.

Your dog can sniff out good times in the lively waters of Crum Creek in the off-leash Crum Woods.

Bonus
In the far southwestern area of campus, beyond the holly collection, is a meadow containing a Swarthmore version of Stonehenge. Like the original, its origins are mysterious. From the slate bench in the middle you can chance to see the SEPTA trolley rolling across a 50-foot trestle over Crum Creek.

Dog Friendliness

Dogs are not only welcomed at Swarthmore, but there are water bowls chained to some of the drinking fountains. In the Crum Woods your dog need only be under voice control, not leashed.

Traffic

A campus walk when school is not in session is a dog-walking pleasure. There will be plenty of streets to cross here, however.

Canine Swimming

Crum Creek is deep enough in many places to permit limited canine swimming.

Trail Time

More than an hour.

Springfield Trail

The Park

The creation of trails in most parks seems fairly obvious - use established animal paths or fire roads. But the *Springfield Trail*, linking four parks in a 5-mile loop roughly corralled by Woodland Avenue, the Blue Route and the SEPTA Trolley line, required vision and imagination of Springfield Township and private property owners in 1969 to bring into existence.

The Walks

There are no shortcuts on the *Springfield Trail*; once you set off you sign on for the whole five miles. The strongest segment is from Jane Lownes Park to Smedley Park as the trail hugs the Crum Creek, often from a scenic ridge 100 feet above the water. Although it's noisy due to the adjacent Blue Route (the trail twice brings you directly beneath the superstructure) this is the walk to take if you decide to do an out-and-back. The hike along the trolley line from Smedley to Thompson Park is a wild and wooly excursion that brings you across train tracks, through dry creek beds, past ferns and wild roses and

Delaware County

Phone Number
- None

Website
- None

Admission Fee
- None

Directions
- *Springfield*; the easiest access is at Lownes Park and Smedley Park. The entrance for Smedley Park is on Baltimore Pike, just east of Exit 2 of the Blue Route. Park in the Paper Mill Road lot across the trolley tracks and pick up the *Trail* at the Comfort Station. Lownes Park is off Route 320 with street parking along Kennerly Road.

The Springfield Trail links four parks where there is always time for a game of stick.

Bonus

The January birthstone: garnets. Mined for thousands of years, the ancients used the stone as bullets for the glowing red color was thought to increase the ferocity of the wound. Legend holds that garnets were carried by travellers to light up the night and protect from nightmares. Noah used a garnet lantern to navigate the Ark at night. Garnets come in every color and can even change hue in different light. And garnets were once mined along Crum Creek here so keep your eyes open on this walk.

more. The quietest stretch on the *Springfield Trail* is the narrow trail along Whiskey Run. There is also sidewalking along Woodland Road to complete the loop. This is a healthy workout; none of the climbs will bring you to your knees but they keep coming with dogged regularity.

Trail Sense: The yellow-blazed trail is well-marked through the woods but can use some touching up in the civilized areas around the trolley tracks and the roads. There is no map so you are dependent on these painted rectangles. The *Springfield Trail* is plagued by trail-obliterating fallen trees; even some of the blazed trees have collapsed into the creek.

Dog Friendliness
Dogs are welcome all along the *Springfield Trail* but there is automobile traffic in places.

Traffic
Although there are many access points to the *Springfield Trail* loop it is possible to achieve a sense of isolation.

Canine Swimming
There are streams everywhere along the *Springfield Trail* but seldom is the water even a foot deep.

Trail Time
Two to three hours to complete the loop; park-to-park segments can be planned for shorter outings.

Springton Manor Park

The Park

Springton Manor was originally an 8,313-acre parcel set aside by William Penn in 1701. The land has been farmed for almost three centuries and lives today as a demonstration farm. A small forge also operated here for much of the 18th century. Abraham McIlvaine built the main house in 1833. Springton Manor Farm is listed on the National Register of Historic Places for its importance in architecture, agriculture and conservation.

Chester County

Phone Number
- (610) 942-2450

Website
- chesco.org/index.aspx?NID=1746

Admission Fee
- None

Directions
- *Glenmoore*; take Route 282, Creek Road, out of Downingtown for five miles and make a left on Springton Road. The entrance to the park is up the hill on the left.

The Walks

The *Indian Run Trail* loops around the entire property - evenly divided between field and woods hiking. In July the southwestern edge of the field is bursting with the most accessible red raspberries in Chester County. There is also available a winding 1/3-mile *Penn Oak Interpretive Nature Trail*. The farmland sweeps down a long hillside providing gentle climbs and sparkling views; the lowlands surrounding Indian Run are flat. The *Indian Run* loop is dirt and grass with some wood chips under foot; the *Nature Trail* is paved with macadam.

Trail Sense: The loop is the only trail on the property. Although it is not marked, it is easy to follow. There is a map available.

"Happiness is dog-shaped."
-Chapman Pincher

> *Bonus*
> **Liberated from their sun-stealing neighbors of the crowded woods, the "King" and "Queen" White Oaks have spread out into a massive canopy of leaves. The "Queen" measures seventeen feet around at the thickest part of the trunk and the "King" is closer to twenty. The two trees are part of the "Penn's Woods" collection of 139 trees standing when William Penn arrived to survey his Pennsylvania colony. The arboreal oldsters reside at the last stop of the nature trail.**

Dog Friendliness
Dogs are welcome along all the trails here.
Traffic
Most likely you will be enjoying the sweeping panoramic views of the countryside by yourself.
Canine Swimming
The Farmer's Pond, at the edge of the *Nature Trail*, was built in 1896 as an additional water source for crops and livestock. The shallow-running Indian Run is good for splashing.
Trail Time
More than an hour.

Your trail dog will find some of the best open-air hiking in southeastern Pennsylvania at Springton Manor.

71

State Game Lands #43

The Park

Three segments of these public lands, totalling 2,150 acres, lie in northwest Chester County. The most accessible - and scenic - of the three is at Saint Peters. Once known as the Falls of French Creek and a famous local tourist destination, Saint Peters was named for the town church when the post office moved away.

The Walks

The *Horse-Shoe Trail* cuts through the Saint Peters and Pine Swamp Tracts. The Saint Peters walk is heavily wooded; the Pine Swamp walk leads through a scruffy meadow on old access roads through light woods at the edge of fields. There are many other short interconnecting trails at Saint Peters, crossing over small streams and an abandoned rail line. The rolling terrain never gets oppressive and the walking is easy throughout, save for a couple of hill pulls.

Trail Sense: The *Horse-Shoe Trail* is blazed but there is no trail map to untwine the maze of trails under the trees at Saint Peters. The *Horse-Shoe Trail* has no branches as it slices through the Pine Swamp tract.

Chester County
Phone Number - None
Website - None
Admission Fee - None
Directions - *Saint Peters*; the parking lot is on Saint Peters Road, north of Route 23 (Ridge Road). It is behind the buildings on the left, at the northern edge of town. In Pine Swamp there is a small, unmarked parking lot on Harmonyville Road, east of Route 345 (Pine Swamp Road).

"What counts is not necessarily the size of the dog in the fight but the size of the fight in the dog."
-Dwight D. Eisenhower

Bonus
**Forty million years ago an igneous explosion
occurred underground here and cooled very quickly
leaving behind a particularly fine granite rock.
Tourists and students of geology alike made the
pilgrimmage to the Falls of French Creek to study
the rock formations. Granite quarries mined the rock
and granite from Saint Peters once received an award
at the 1893 World's Columbian Exposition in Chicago
as "a fine-grained polished cube, a good building and
ornamental stone." The quarries closed in the 1960s
and many pits can still be seen. Today the giant boulders
in French Creek are ideal for your dog to scramble
on - or just lie in the sun.**

**The best canine swimming hole in the Delaware Valley
comes with launching pads in the form of boulders.**

Dog Friendliness
Dogs are welcome along all the trails here.

Traffic
Save for maps, there is nothing to lead visitors to this parcel of Pennsylvania state game lands. No signs, no mapboards. You should have these woods to yourself.

Canine Swimming
French Creek rushes downhill through the property, pooling into an ideal swimming pond just south of the parking lot. Pine Creek can be accessed at Pine Swamp from the bridge near the parking lot.

Trail Time
More than one hour available.

Tamanend Community Park

The Park

In an elaborate treaty ceremony in his Philadelphia house in 1683, William Penn purchased all the land between Pennypack and Neshaminy Creeks. In turning over the lands, Chief Tamanend, a Lenape Sachem, declared the treaty of friendship would endure "as long as the grass is green and the rivers flow." Scarcely a half century later Penn's descendents had bro-ken the treaty and driven the Lenape nation from Pennsylvania. A wooden figurehead likeness of Chief Tamanend graced the *USS Delaware* and eventually wound up on the grounds of the United States Naval Academy.

Bucks County

Phone Number
- (215) 355-9781

Website
- None

Admission Fee
- None

Directions
- *Southampton*; entrance is on Second Street Pike (Route 232) between Bristol Road and Street Road (Route 132).

This land was farmed for more than two centuries until the 1940s when William Long established Southampton Nurseries. In addition to the commercial stock, Long introduced exotic species of trees and shrubs as well. In 1975 Upper Southampton Township and the Centennial School District jointly purchased the 109-acre Tamanend Park for nearly one million dollars.

The Walks

For a small township park wedged between a rail line and a busy roadway, Tamanend sports a surprising variety of canine hikes. The *Red Arrowhead Trail* skirts the perimeter of the property for 2.3 miles and the *Blue Arrowhead* and *Yellow Arrowhead* trails are interior loops of about one mile in length. The dirt trails are generally wide and easy to negotiate.

Two short, special trails are the stars at Tamanend, however. The *History Trail* interprets the heritage of the property and structures remaining

Bonus
**The Glade is a special garden designed to
spotlight a thick-trunked European Beech Tree,
the Cedars of Lebanon and a giant Red Oak
with thick, twisting wisteria vines climbing all the way
to the crown. Set apart in the grass are Sweetbay
Magnolia trees and two ancient Southern Magnolia trees.
In a back corner of the Glade is the Butterfly Garden with
plantings selected to attract butterflies.**

from by-gone days. Highlights include the William Penn Treaty Elm, a fifth generation offspring of the great elm tree under which Penn negotiated with the Lenni Lenape, and a Sequoia *Giganteum*, a species of mountain redwood originally found only in China and California. The *Glenn Sokol Trail* is a quiet nature trail created in honor of a local naturalist.

Trail Sense: Tamanend is not for the directionally-challenged. Although there are rudimentary maps and trails are blazed, the primary tool for getting around Tamanend is printed turn-by-turn directions in the trail brochures.

Dog Friendliness
All trails are open to dogs.
Traffic
This is a compact, busy park and the trails touch on many of the recreation areas in the park.
Canine Swimming
There is some dog paddling to be had in the small Klinger Pond but this is not a canine swimmer's paradise.
Trail Time
More than an hour.

Taylor Arboretum

The Park

The ownership of this property dates to William Penn who sold a thousand-acre land grant to John Sharpless in 1682. Sharpless descendents operated grist and cotton mills here for nearly two centuries. Taylor Memorial Arboretum was established in 1931 by a Chester lawyer, Joshua C. Taylor, in the memory of his wife, Anne Rulon Gray.

The Walks

The many trails through these 30 acres along Ridley Creek are short, interconnecting segments about evenly divided between woods and meadow. There are many highlights here, including plant-covered rock outcroppings, a bald cypress pond, and a groundwater spring. There is some slope on the property down to the floodplain of the Ridley Creek but the walking is easy. The trail surfaces are soft dirt and grass and pine straw.

Delaware County

Phone Number
- (610) 876-2649

Website
- taylorarboretum.org

Admission Fee
- None

Directions
- *Wallingford*; from I-95 take Exit 6 and follow Route 320 North. Just past 22nd Street, make a left on Chestnut Parkway and continue to the Arboretum entrance, making a left on Ridley Drive.

The displays in the arboretum make a sensuous backdrop to your dog's hike.

Bonus
**The Taylor Memorial Arboretum provides a
12-Tree Self-Guided Tour. The collection is especially
strong in Far Eastern specimens and spotlights three
Pennsylvania State Champion trees: the Needle Juniper,
the Lacebark Elm and the Giant Dogwood.
Also on the tour is a Dawn Redwood,
an ancient tree known only through fossils until
1941 when a botany student tracked down living
specimens in rural China. Some of the first seed to
come to America resulted in this tree.**

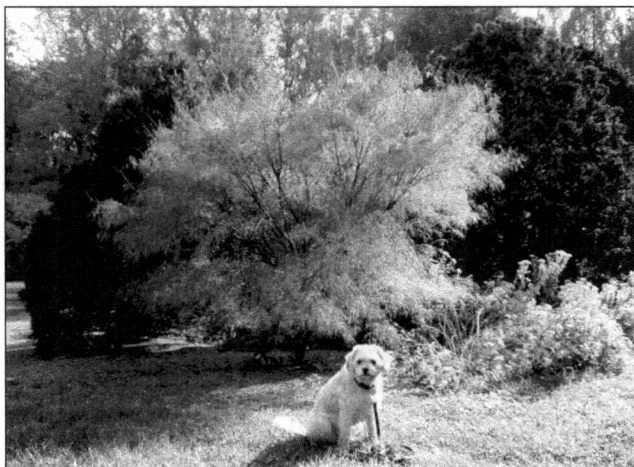

**The Taylor Arboretum is home to several
Pennsylvania State Champion trees.**

Trail Sense: The trails are not blazed but a detailed site map is available. There is also a map board at the parking lot.

Dog Friendliness

Dogs can enjoy the views from the Green Knob lookout tower.

Traffic

Foot traffic only.

Canine Swimming

None.

Trail Time

Less than one hour to climb to the tower and return to the Parkway.

Tyler
State Park

The Park

The rolling lands along the Neshaminy Creek here have supported a vibrant farming community for over 300 years. Some of the stone dwellings peppered around the property date to the early 1700s. Funding from Pennsylvania conservation programs resulted in the opening of Tyler State Park in 1974. Today, more than 400 of the park's 1,711 acres are still under cultivation.

The Walks

Neshaminy Creek bisects Tyler State Park into two distinctly differ-

Bucks County

Phone Number
- (215) 968-2021

Website
- dcnr.state.pa.us/stateparks/find-apark/tyler

Admission Fee
- None

Directions
- *Newtown*; from I-95 at the Newtown/Yardley Exit 49, drive west on the four-lane bypass around Newtown. The park entrance is on the left at the intersection of Swamp Road and the four-lane bypass.

With all the trails at Tyler State Park your dog will appreciate a break every now and then.

Bonus
In the farthest northern section of Tyler State Park is the longest covered bridge in Bucks County. The 117-year old Schofield Ford Covered Bridge burned in 1991 but after five years of fundraising the 166-foot, two-span crossing was entirely rebuilt by volunteers on its original stone abutments using authentic period materials and methods.

ent halves. The eastern side is distinguished by a tightly bunched network of gravel hiking paths connecting the popular recreational areas located in this section of the park. The trails are shady and hilly.

Across the creek, the trails stretch out for longer walks. There are more than ten miles of paved multi-purpose bicycle trails and almost as many miles of dirt-and-grass bridle paths. The trail system, one of the most elaborate in greater Philadelphia, can be customized into an endless array of short or long hikes. The terrain remains hilly, especially on the steep, self-guiding nature trail that loops its way around Parker Run as it feeds into Neshaminy Creek.

Trail Sense: In the western section of Tyler State Park the trails are named at their junctions and a detailed park map is available.

Dog Friendliness
Dogs are welcome on all trails in the park.
Traffic
Tyler is a busy place, pulsing with scores of walkers, cyclists and equestrians. The further you push from the heart of the park, the lighter the traffic becomes. There are parking lots near the outer perimeter of the park that permit access to the more remote trails.
Canine Swimming
The Neshaminy Creek is an excellent venue for canine aquatics with many access points from the trail above the dam.
Trail Time
You can spend the better part of a half-day with your dog on Tyler State Park trails if you desire.

"My dog can bark like a Congressman, fetch like an aide, beg like a press secretary and play dead like a receptionist."
-Gerald Solomon

Valley Forge National Historic Park

The Park

The most famous name in the American Revolution comes to us from a small iron forge built along Valley Creek in the 1740s. No battles were fought here, but during the winter of 1777-78, when Valley Forge grew to be the third largest city in America, hundreds of soldiers died from sickness and disease. America's attention was redirected to long-forgotten Valley Forge during a Centennial in 1878. Preservation efforts began with Washington's Headquarters and evolved into the National Park.

The Walks

These are some of the most historic walks in America and some of the most beautiful in greater Philadelphia - panoramic vistas from rolling hills, long waterside hikes and climbs up

Chester County

Phone Number
- (610) 783-1000

Website
- nps.gov/vafo/

Admission Fee
- None

Directions
- *Valley Forge*; the main park entrance is on Route 23 off Route 422. Parking for the Valley Creek Trail is on Route 252 (although the Foot Bridge is washed out as of this writing). To reach the Schuylkill River Trail, exit from Route 422 onto Trooper Road, make a left and continue back across Route 422 to the Betzwood Picnic Area or cross the Schuylkill River on Pawlings Road from Route 23 at the other end. Parking for trails here is on the right side across the bridge and also up the road at Walnut Hill.

wooded mountainsides. There are four marked trails, plus miles of unmarked hikes. The paved *Multi-Use Trail* loops the Colonial defensive lines and Grand Parade Ground and visits George Washington's headquarters. Sweeping field scenes are found all along the trail's six-mile length. The *Valley Creek Trail* is a flat, linear 1.2 mile walk along Valley Creek, past the Upper Forge site. Near the Valley Creek is the eastern terminus of the 133-mile *Horse-Shoe Trail*; the journey to the *Appalachian Trail* in Hershey begins at the Artificer's Shops on Route 23. The *Horse-Shoe Trail* demands a steep and strenuous climb up Mount Misery, the natural southern defender of

Bonus

The *Multi-Use Trail* rolls past reconstructed huts and parade grounds that transport you back to the Revolution. The National Memorial Arch, a massive stone tribute dedicated in 1917, stands out along the route. The inscription reads: "Naked and starving as they are, we cannot enough admire the incomparable patience and fidelity of the soldiery. Washington at Valley Forge, February 16, 1778."

Washington's encampment that will test even your athletic dog. Across the Schuylkill River is the 3-mile linear *Schuylkill River Trail* connecting the Pawling's Parking Area and the Betzwood Picnic Area. The flat dirt trail hugs the river the entire way.

Trail Sense: A National Park Service map provides locations for the trails and does not indicate the variety of side trails available, especially from the *Schuylkill River Trail*.

Dog Friendliness

Dogs are welcome on all the trails here.

Traffic

Valley Forge is popular with dog walkers, cyclists and joggers but there is relief from the crowds at Valley Forge on the unmarked dirt trails at Walnut Hill across the Schuylkill River, off Pawlings Road.

Canine Swimming

Valley Creek is a delightful watering hole and the Schuylkill River is easily accessed for hardcore swimming canines.

Trail Time

Budget at least an hour regardless of what division you explore with your best trail companion at Valley Forge.

Warwick
County Park

The Park

The woodlands in Warwick County Park's 455 acres provided much of the timber for charcoal used in the American iron industry. The land was an original grant to Samuel Nutt in 1718, who took to mining the property. By 1738 the Warwick Furnace was established and it was to be one of the most substantial in the American colonies. The first Franklin Stove was cast here and the Warwick Cannon helped win the Revolution. Charcoal hearths chiseled into the steep slopes can still be seen flanking some trails. The park was dedicated in 1973.

Chester County

Phone Number
- (610) 469-1916

Website
- chesco.org/index.aspx?NID=1747

Admission Fee
- None

Directions
- *Knauertown*; on Route 23, four miles west of Route 100. The main park entrance is located on County Park Road and parking for the North Loop Trail is on Mt. Pleasant Road, east of the main entrance.

The Walks

The premier walk in Warwick is the *Charcoal Trail Loop*, a narrow, rocky, mile-long loop up and down the slopes of the French Creek Valley. The *North Loop Trail*, designed like a long lasso, is a pleasant woods-and-field walk, much of it on the old bed of the Sowbelly Railroad. Two of the *Horse-Shoe Trail's* 133 miles bisect the park and there is a 1/2-mile *Adirondack Trail* where you can test your ability to identify the trees and shrubs commonly found in an Eastern hardwood forest. The trail access from the Coventry Road parking lot is overgrown and provides access only to the French Creek South Branch, but not the rest of the park. There are many long stretches of flat terrain and easy walking but the *Charcoal Trail* will give your dog a cardiac workout.

Bonus

In 1850 Albert Fink, a German railroad engineer, designed and patented a bridge that used a latticework of rods instead of cables to reinforce stiffness. This construction was cheap and sturdy, making the Fink Truss one of the most commonly used railroad bridges in the 1860s, especially favored by the powerful Baltimore & Ohio Railroad. Only one Fink Truss bridge remains in the United States - an abandoned 108-foot span in Zoarsville, Ohio. A wooden reproduction of a Fink Truss is in a field at Warwick County Park for you and your dog to climb.

Trail Sense: The trails are blazed, save for the *North Loop*, and a trail map is available.

Dog Friendliness
Dogs are welcome along all the trails here.

Traffic
The trails won't be clogged in this park in rural Chester County.

Canine Swimming
There is very little water at Warwick; none at all along the *Charcoal Trail* and minimal access to the French Creek elsewhere. There is, however, a pretty, fleeting encounter with the creek on the *North Loop*, west of the Conifer Field.

Trail Time
More than an hour.

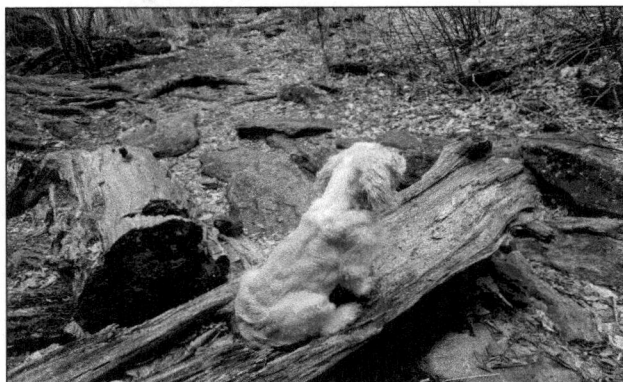

Taking a break along the trail in Warwick woods.

Welkinweir

The Park

Welkinweir ("where sky meets water") was a foundering farm during the Depression when the property was purchased by Everett and Grace Rodebaugh. The Rodebaughs reintroduced native trees and meadows and constructed a series of ponds in the valley beneath the farmhouse.

In 1964, Everett Rodebaugh founded the Green Valleys Association to protect five watersheds draining 151 square miles of northern Chester County. In 1997 the Rodebaughs conveyed Welkinweir to the Green Valleys Association for use as a headquarters and educational center.

The Walks

A woodland trail loops around the 162-acre nature sanctuary, leading through wetlands, ponds, and meadows. The trail, which takes about an hour to complete, can be narrow and overgrown through the back of the property. For longer walks, the Welkinweir trail features a short connector to the *Horse-Shoe Trail*, which skirts the property on two sides.

This is hilly property, especially in the backstretch of the loop. Some

Chester County

Phone Number
- (610) 469-4990

Website
- greenvalleys.org/welk.html

Admission Fee
- Adults (17 & up) - $5.00;
  Youth - $3.00

Directions
- *Phoenixville*; west of town. From the intersection of Routes 23 and 100, take Route 100 south for 1.1 miles. Make a right on Prizer Road. Follow for .8 a mile to Welkinweir on the left. The Visitor Entrance is the second of three access points and is marked by a sign.

Bonus
There are dramatic vistas from the garden areas around the property. As one visitor commented in the Welkinweir guest book: "It's a Grand Canyon of trees!"

of the meadow trails are shaved stalks which are rough on your pet's paws.

Trail Sense: The *West Trail* entrance begins at the parking lot and the trail is blazed in white. It is not a complete loop and there is a property map available to navigate through the developed areas.

Dog Friendliness
Dogs are welcome along all the trails here.

Traffic
The small admission fee at Welkinweir helps keep crowds down.

Canine Swimming
Although the West Branch of Beaver Run is not deep enough for doggie dipping, it engorges into several ponds on the property.

Trail Time
More than an hour.

There is plenty for your dog to see during a day at Welkinweir.

The 50 Best Places
To Hike With Your Dog
Around Philadelphia...

Delaware

Alapocas Run State Park

The Park

The original 123 acres of the 145-acre park were deeded to Wilmington in 1910 by William Poole Bancroft, founder of the city's park system. Today, Alapocas is a part of Wilmington State Parks, although the gate on the bridge connecting the park to Rockford Park is locked more often than not.

The Walks

The main *Alapocas Woods Trail* tumbles up and down wooded hillsides for 1.8 miles. After a narrow start (a new trail segment), the path is wide, the trees are mature with little understory to block your views and the canine hiking is splendid. Most of the way, including side loops like the *Paw-Paw Trail* (that is the tree, not a dogs-only trail), the footpaths are covered in paw-friendly dirt.

> ### New Castle County
>
> **Phone Number**
> - (302) 577-1164
>
> **Website**
> - destateparks.com/park/alapocas-run
>
> **Admission Fee**
> - None
>
> **Directions**
> - *Wilmington*; behind the DuPont Experimental Station, off Route 141 on Alapocas Drive. The trailhead is in the woods at the back of the parking lot. You can also access the trails from Alapocas Drive.

If, however, you venture off the main track and hike down to the Brandywine River you will do so on a steep, rocky track that is hard on foot and paw. Your reward for this exploration is a descent into the industrial heritage of the river. As you walk along the water you will be in the shadow of the Bancroft Mills complex, once the largest cotton finishing works in the world. The path in this section of the park becomes flat and paved and you can return to the *Alapocas Woods Trail* on smooth macadam if you so choose.

Trail Sense: There is a mapboard and signposts on the trails, but not at every intersection.

Bonus
Squeezed between the Piedmont and coastal plain zones, Alapocas offers some of the most dramatic geology in Delaware. The granite cliffs here are high enough to claim the state's only natural waterfall and plentiful enough for the Brandywine Granite Company to have once quarried over 600,000 tons of Wilmington "Blue Rocks" from this site between 1883 and 1888.

The remnants of a century-old quarry make a striking background for your dog's adventures in Alapocas Run State Park along the Brandywine River.

Dog Friendliness
Keep your dog off the ballfields and let her romp in the woods.

Traffic
There is little competition for these trails.

Canine Swimming
There is fun to be had in the rapids between large boulders and lazy dog paddling in the slower stretches of the Brandywine River.

Trail Time
You can spend about an hour on these trails and in the river.

Ashland
Nature Center

The Park

A mill operated here as early as 1715. Since 1964, when the Delaware Nature Society was founded, 130 acres at Ashland Nature Center have been preserved for the conservation and study of natural resources.

The Walks

There are four self-guiding nature trails here, each a loop between .8 and 1.3 miles. *Sugarbush* and *Treetop* trails explore the wooded hillside beyond the Ashland Covered Bridge, built in the days before the Civil War; the

New Castle County
Phone Number - (302) 239-2334
Website - delawarenaturesociety.org/ashland.htm
Admission Fee - Yes, to use the trails
Directions - *Hockessin*; on Barley Mill Road, between Creek Road (Route 82) and Brackenville Road.

adjoining *Succession* and *Flood Plain* trails visit meadow, marsh, pond and forest. There is a good deal of hillwalking at Ashland, save for the benign *Flood Plain Trail*. The trails are natural - dirt covered in the woods; grass in the meadows.

Trail Sense: The trails and interpretive stops, over 30 on some trails, are well-marked. Detailed brochures are available in the kiosk at the parking lot.

Dog Friendliness
Dogs are welcome at the Ashland Nature Center.
Traffic
No bikes or horses compete on the trails; expect group nature tours,though.
Canine Swimming
Birch Run and the Red Clay Creek flow through the property. Neither is deep enough to dog paddle in.
Trail Time
More than one hour.

This is where you can find the answers to all those
questions that confound you when
walking in other northern Delaware parks:
1. Why is this park so hilly?
Glacial runoff carved Delaware's valleys from a high plateau.
2. What are the dominant trees in these woods?
Oak and beech.
3. How did all this sand get in this creek?
Eroded soil carried downstream from far-off mountains.
4. Where did all these big rocks come from?
*Schists of rock were folded in by
intense pressure deep in the earth.*
5. Why do these trees grow so tall, straight and branchless?
*The trees, usually tulip poplars that compete with sycamores
as the burliest in Eastern forests, are shade intolerant
and are constantly striving for the sun.*

**The Ashland Covered Bridge is a link for your dog to
use on the trail system around the nature center.**

*"If you pick up a starving dog and make him prosperous,
he will not bite you; that is the principal
difference between a dog and a man."*
-Mark Twain

Bellevue
State Park

The Park

Bellevue is the former estate of William du Pont, Jr., one of Delaware's greatest sportsmen. Here he stabled his Foxcatcher Farms horses and five Kentucky Derby horses worked on the training track now used by cyclists and joggers. He brought pari-mutuel racing to Delaware and designed Delaware Park racetrack. As president of the Wilmington Country Club he donated the golf course's original holes to the city of Wilmington for the Porky Oliver Golf Course. The tennis courts at Bellevue were one of the greatest private tennis complexes ever when du Pont hosted international stars at his famous "tennis Sundays." He married one of America's greatest court stars, Margaret Osbourne, in 1947. Bellevue became a 328-acre state park in 1976, ten years after William du Pont's death.

New Castle County

Phone Number
- (302) 761-6963

Website
- destateparks.com/park/bellevue

Admission Fee
- Yes, May to October

Directions
- *Claymont*; the main entrance is on Carr Road, between Marsh Road (Exit 9 off I-95) and Silverside Road.

The Walks

The main attraction for hikers at Bellevue is the 9-furlong (1 1/8 miles) training track. It is wide, flat and exceedingly pleasant to walk. Unfortunately for canine hikers, in recent years the dirt track has been covered in crushed stone and dogs have been banned. Your dog can still trot on the grass shoulder, however.

You can also cobble together a canine hike around the perimeter of the park by following paved bike paths and unpaved horse trails. These lead to community gardens, a small nature preserve, the historic paddocks and estate buildings.

Trail Sense: A park mapboard is available at the parking lot.

Bonus
When William du Pont took over the property he transformed a Gothic Revival castle into a graceful replica of President James Madison's home, Montpelier. It is now the centerpiece of the park.

The Neoclassical William du Pont mansion lords over the manicured grounds in Bellevue State Park.

Dog Friendliness

Dogs are welcome in the park but not on the main training track.

Traffic

You will always find folks using the training track but there is plenty of room to stretch out.

Canine Swimming

There is a small fishing pond that is reserved for fishing, not dog paddling.

Trail Time

It will take more than an hour to fully explore the grounds of one of Delaware's great estates.

Brandywine Creek State Park

The Park

Once a du Pont family dairy farm, this spectacular swath of land became a State Park in 1965. Delaware's first two nature preserves are located here: Tulip Tree Woods, behind the park office, and Freshwater Marsh, at the edge of Brandywine Creek. The stone walls that criss-cross the 850-acre park are the legacy of skilled Italian masons who crafted the barriers from locally quarried Brandywine granite - the original "Wilmington Blue Rocks."

The Walks

There are eight blazed trails totalling 14 miles on both sides of the Brandywine Creek. All are short, all are woodsy and if you can't reach out and touch the water you are moving up or down a hill. The *Hidden Pond Trail* and the *Indian Springs Trail* each travel along the water, immerse you in the steep valley terrain and traverse the Tulip Tree Woods, where majestic tulip poplar have grown for nearly two centuries.

The star walk at Thompson's Bridge is the rugged, 1.9-mile *Rocky Run Trail*, winding around the closest thing to a mountain stream in Delaware. On this trail you'll discover fragrant stands of hemlock nestled among hardwood neighbors in a mature forest with long views. Nearby, the *Multi-Use Trail* tags Brandywine Creek for the better part of two miles.

Check with the park office about programs that welcome well-behaved dogs. Your dog can experience such events as a Civil War re-enactment or star-gazing from the open fields.

New Castle County

Phone Number
- (302) 577-3534

Website
- destateparks.com/park/brandy-wine-creek

Admission Fee
- Yes, May to October

Directions
- *Wilmington*; The main entrance is on Adams Dam Road, between Thompson's Bridge Road (Route 92) and Rockland Road. Other parking areas are at Thompson's Bridge and off Rockland Road, opposite Rockland Mills.

Bonus
In the winter of 1802 a rudderless French immigrant living in New Jersey named Eleuthere Irenee du Pont was invited to the Brandywine Valley to hunt game. It was not a successful trip. The damp weather fouled his gunpowder so that his musket continually misfired. It was so bad du Pont decided to re-enter the industry he had turned his back on in France as a youth: black powder. When it came time to launch his new business he remembered what you see today at Brandywine Creek State Park - the hardwood forests that would burn to charcoal, one of the ingredients he would need for powder; the abundant granite in the hills to build his mills; and the swift-flowing river to power the mills. And so he returned to Delaware to found a dynasty. Incidentally, the favorite breed of dog for the du Pont family when they lived here: the greyhound.

Trail Sense: All the paths are blazed and there is a map available. There are some unblazed trails in the Thompson's Bridge area but you can figure out where you are headed.

Dog Friendliness

Dogs are welcome to share the trails in all sections of the park.

Traffic

Brandywine Creek State Park is a heavily-used park; bikes are restricted to the *Multi-Use Trail*.

Canine Swimming

The Brandywine Creek is one of the best places in Delaware to take your dog for a swim. There is plenty of access to the water from the low banks in the main park.

Trail Time

Brandywine Creek State Park can host an all-day outing or a quick loop with your dog.

The Brandywine Creek is the best place to take your water-loving dog in Delaware.

Carousel Park

The Park

Carousel Park is another legacy to recreation in Delaware from the du Pont family, being a former family estate. Long the home of public riding stables, New Castle County has worked to make the park a mecca for hiking as well.

The Walks

Carousel is a suburban park given over to walking - no playgrounds or ballfields here. The main trail (*The Carousel Loop*) is a three-mile walk around the circumference of the park. Many short connecting trails dissect the park as well. All told their are 14 trails in the park winding through open fields, horse pastures, ponds, hardwoods (Land of the Giants) and pine trees (Sherwood Forest). Carousel Park is set in rolling hills; a healthy climb is required to reach Strawberry Field in the back of the park. The *Carousel Loop* is covered with paw-pleasing wood chips the entire way while the connecting trails are gravel roads, dirt and sometimes grass.

Trail Sense: The trails are all well-marked, color-coded and sport whimsical names. Locator map boards are also on site.

New Castle County

Phone Number
- None

Website
- None

Admission Fee
- None

Directions
- *Wilmington*; the main parking lot for Carousel Park, halfway between Newark and Wilmington, is on Limestone Road (Route 7) between Milltown Road and New Linden Hill Road. Smaller parking lots are at the end of Old Linden Hill Road, off Limestone Road, and on Skyline Drive, off New Linden Hill Road.

Bonus
**An off-leash Bark Park at Carousel Park has been
established in an open field above Enchanted Lake.
For dogs who enjoy a refreshing dip,
this is the place to come.**

Dog Friendliness

Carousel Park is one of the most popular places to bring dogs in northern Delaware.

Traffic

There are plenty of walkers, joggers and other dogs on the trails.

Canine Swimming

A trail encircles Enchanted Lake, an ideal spot for canine aquatics with easy access to the water from the banks. Another smaller swimming hole is the less fashionable Moonlight Pond.

Trail Time

More than one hour.

**Swimming will be on the menu when
you come to explore Carousel Park.**

Middle Run Valley Natural Area

The Park

The White Clay Creek drains some 70,000 acres and 100 square miles in Pennsylvania and Delaware. In Delaware, where Middle Run is one of its three main tributaries, it seems that much of that watershed is choked by suburban sprawl. Beginning in 1975, local civic and environmental groups began piece-meal acquisition of pristine woodlands that has resulted in an 850-acre oasis in the center of housing subdivisions, shopping centers and busy roadways.

New Castle County

Phone Number
- None

Website
- None

Admission Fee
- None

Directions
- *Newark*; northeast of town. From Kirkwood Highway (Route 2) follow Possum Park Road 1.7 miles to Possum Hollow Road on the right. Take a left at the entrance to the park after about 1/2 mile.

The Walks

Middle Run features splendid canine hiking on five well-maintained loop trails that cover 14 miles and an additional five short spurs that lead to surrounding communites. All offer interesting - and sometimes challenging - switches in terrain. There is almost 200 feet of elevation change at Middle Run.

The purple-blazed *Lenape Trail* visits most of the property in its run of almost 7 miles, one of the longest loop trails in Delaware. The best choice for dog walkers only wanting to sample Middle Run's sylvan charms is the pedestrian-only 2.15-mile *Possum Hollow Trail*. Another good ramble is the *Earth Day Trail* that drops out of the parking lot into a steep valley around Muddy Run.

All the natural dirt and grass trails bound up and down hills but the *Snow Geese Trail*, marked in orange on the east side of the park, is an especially steep, heart-pumping loop for canine and human.

Bonus

The patches of long-abandoned farmland are good places to spot hawks. Hawks can appear at Middle Run at any time of the year but in fall and spring the skies overflow with migrating hawks making long-distance trips between their breeding grounds and winter residences. Fall migration usually begins in mid-August and continues through late November. Spring migration takes place between March and May.

Trail Sense: The trails are not continually blazed but markers direct the way at trail junctions. New Castle County publishes a superb trail map and brochure but it is available only in county offices, not at the park. The map board at the Possum Hollow Road parking lot is the best in the state to help guide you.

Dog Friendliness
Dogs are welcome on all trails.

Traffic
Even though the parking lot has room for only 24 cars, it seems frivilously large most of the time. No one stumbles upon Middle Run. There are no directional signs announcing its existence from any of the major roads enclosing this natural area. Expect little company on these trails although there is an active community of mountain bikers that ride here.

Canine Swimming
There are no ponds on the property and the Middle Run and its branches are too shallow for swimming. There is enough water, however, for splashing on a hot day.

Trail Time
There are many hours of canine hiking here.

Every step of the way is through woods at Middle Run so your dog will have plenty of chances to find a prize stick.

White Clay Creek State Park/Preserve

The Park

William Penn bought most of this land in 1683 from Lenni Lenape Chief Kekelappen, who was believed to have lived here in Opasiskunk, the most important of the region's "Indian Towns." In 1968 White Clay Creek began life as a state park with 24 statepurchased acres of land. In 1984 the DuPont Company donated the land that would be the foundation for today's park of 3,384 acres with another 1,253 adjoining acres across the state line in Pennsylvania.

The Walks

White Clay serves up the widest menu of canine hiking choices of any park in the First State - almost 40 miles of trails on a dozen marked trails. The top choices in the Walter S. Carpenter, Jr. Recreation Area are the hardy 5-mile *Twin Valley Trail* and the sporty 2-mile *Millstone Trail* with its scenic rock outcroppings and two never-finished millstones. A half-mile *Logger's Trail* illuminates the history of lumbering in the area.

The only trail that actually visits the White Clay Creek is the *Penndel Trail*, over three miles in length, connecting the park and the preserve. It is a superb linear trail for hiking with your dog - flat for its entire length and uniformly wide. Nearby, at the park office on Thompson Station Road, is a trailhead for a rugged hill climb on the homesite of David English, a lease

New Castle County

Phone Number
- (302) 368-6900

Website
- destateparks.com/park/white-clay-creek

Admission Fee
- Yes, May-October

Directions
- *Newark*; The main parking lot is in the Walter Carpenter, Jr. Recreation Area on New London Road (Route 896), three miles northwest of Newark. Parking is also available on Hopkins Road at the Chambers House Nature Center, on Chamber Rock Road and the end of Thompson Station Road at the Park Office. Possum Hill is located off Paper Mill Road (Route 72) between Polly Drummond Road and Possum Park Road. The Judge Morris Estate is on Polly Drummond Road.

Bonus

To visit White Clay Creek is to indulge in a lesson of American surveying history. The *Twin Valley Trail* swings past the Arc Corner Monument marking one end of the 12-mile arc that forms the Pennsylvania-Delaware state line, unique in American political boundary making. The circular divide dates to William Penn's directive of August 28, 1701. A half-mile to the west there is a monument marking the tri-state junction of Delaware, Pennsylvania and Maryland. Over at Possum Hill, tucked back in the woods, is a small cement pillar. This post was set up - facing west - in Alexander Bryan's field on June 12, 1764 by English mathematicians Charles Mason and Jeremiah Dixon. This base point, 15 miles south of the southernmost point of the city of Philadelphia, began the survey for the Mason-Dixon Line that would forever separate North from South.

holder of the William Penn family.

While you are warming up for hill climbs, visit Possum Hill, where two stacked loop trails fall 150 feet among thick stands of mature beech and oaks that thrive in the moist valleys. The scenery on the 2-mile *Long Loop* is more arresting so save the inner loop for a second go-round.

The fourth - and newest - section of White Clay Creek was acquired in 1998 at the Judge Morris Estate. Along with an elegant 1790s mansion the park annexed one of the finest loop trails in the state. The 3-mile ramble is wooded throughout and dips and rolls across tumbling terrain. The path is narrow, however, and a favorite of mountain bikers.

Trail Sense: The paths are blazed, the paths are named and there is an excellent color map available. But some stretches share two or three trails so pay attention.

Dog Friendliness
Dogs are welcome to share the trails in all sections of the park.
Traffic
For a canine hike less traveled, try Possum Hill or the Judge Morris Estate.
Canine Swimming
The swift and shallow White Clay Creek is the purest around for drinking. Occasional pools host some dog paddling and there are farm ponds in the park.
Trail Time
A half-day and more is possible.

Wilmington State Parks

The Park

Brandywine Park, Delaware's first park, created in 1885 and partially designed by Frederick Law Olmsted, can stand beside any of America's downtown riverwalks for person and dog. The 178-acre park of wooded trails, formal gardens, and sculptures was added to the National Historic Register in 1976.

Rockford Park dates to 1889, when there were still fears of visitors being harmed by explosions in the DuPont Company black powder yards down the street. William Poole Bancroft began his life-long efforts to preserve open space in the Brandywine Valley here, with a gift of 59 acres. Today the park comprises 104 acres. The two city parks have been linked by a footpath and joined under a Delaware state park umbrella.

New Castle County

Phone Number
- (302) 577-7020

Website
- destateparks.com/park/wilmington

Admission Fee
- None

Directions
- *Wilmington*; the main parking lot for Brandywine Park is on the north banks of the river at the foot of Monkey Hill, off of 18th and Van Buren streets. The entrances to Rockford Park are at 19th Street and Tower Road and Riverview Avenue and Red Oak Road.

The Walks

The 1.8-mile *Brandywine Nature Trail* connects Brandywine Village and Rockford Park. Through Brandywine Park it traces the north shore of the Brandywine River for about a mile.

Once across the Swinging Bridge, the trail veers away from the water towards Rockford Park via Kentmere Parkway. Along the way you'll enjoy native and ornamental plantings in the Rose Garden, the Waterwalk Garden, the Four Seasons Garden, the historic Josephine Gardens and elsewhere. Under paw will be concrete sidewalk and macadam on this canine hike.

Bonus

Rockford Park is home to one of the Delaware's most cherished and recognized landmarks - the 115-foot Rockford Tower. The Italian Renaissance Revival style tower, designed by Theodore Leisen, engineer for the Wilmington Board of Park Commissioners, was built on what was called Mt. Salem Hill, the highest point in the city at 330 feet above sea level and completed in 1902. The beautiful natural field stone tower encloses a steel water tank holding 500,000 gallons of water. The Observatory at the top was once a popular tourist destination but closed during repairs in 1972. For the tower's centennial in 2002 the Observatory re-opened and visitors can once again climb the 132 steps to the top weekends from May to October.

The main walk at Rockford Park is along the circular road through the property but there are narrow, informal trails in the woods that run in parallel terraces around the steep hill, including one on an old rail bed.

You can sculpt a canine hike by circling the road up top and introduce a hill by descending "Sledding Hill." You can also hike through the woods down to the Brandywine River. Other options include the connecting path to Brandywine Park or across the river to Alapocas Woods, providing the gate is open.

Trail Sense: Mapboards are scattered through the park.

Dog Friendliness
Three areas within Wilmington State Parks are managed as "off leash" areas for dogs. Two are located in Brandywine Park and one in Rockford Park.

Traffic
This is a go-to destination for Wilmington dog owners.

Canine Swimming
Dogs can enjoy a dip in the Brandywine River and in the mill race cut on the south side. In 1954, the Brandywine Canoe Slalom, America's first ever slalom race for kayaks, ran in these waters south of the Washington Street bridge. Two decades later water kayaking would become a popular Olympic sport.

Trail Time
Anything from a quick social visit at the dog park to a hike of an hour or more.

Woodlawn Trustees Property

The Park

From 1850 until 1910, feldspar, used in porcelain dishes and false teeth, was mined here in the Woodlawn Quarry. You can still see the remains of these spar pits, with their scatterings of mica and other minerals. In 1910, as his campaign to preserve the Brandywine Valley intensified, William Poole Bancroft bought hundreds of pristine acres in the lush floodplain and rolling woodlands where the Brandywine Creek makes three wide, gentle turns. Bancroft formed the Woodlawn Company to manage these lands, harboring some of the oldest trees in Delaware. Today, more than 2,000 acres are open to the public for recreational use - one of the greatest private gifts to canine hikers to be found anywhere.

The Walks

These informal dirt trails through a mix of open fields and mature forests can be combined to create any kind of day out with your dog. Athletic dogs will enjoy bounding along the grassy hillsides above the Brandywine. Walking back and forth on the *Fire Trail* along the water provides an easy

New Castle County

Phone Number
- None

Website
- None

Admission Fee
- None

Directions
- *Wilmington*; there are no highway signs to direct you here and the parking lots are not marked.
The main parking lot is opposite Peters Rock along the Brandywine on Creek Road. Other gravel lots can be found on Ramsey Road, Beaver Valley Road and opposite Woodlawn Road on Thompson's Bridge Road (Route 92). There is also parking in the hotel complex on Route 202.

A day on the Woodlawn Property hills is sure to unleash the inner farm dog in your best trail buddy.

Bonus
**Breaking out of the woods at several points on the
hilltops you are greeted with splendid views
of Granogue, one of the American castles dotting the
Brandywine Valley's chateau lands.**

45-minute walk.

The trails can be jumping off points for hikes of several hours duration. Following the white blazes of the Wilmington Trail Club along the creek you can reach Chadds Ford. You can ford Beaver Valley Road into Pennsylvania and loop around the fast-flowing Beaver Run. The route is hilly and requires some careful creek crossings but is very scenic. Finally you

**The Woodlawn trails trip across
the Brandywine Valley's
celebrated Chateau Country.**

can cross Thompson's Bridge Road and walk into Brandywine Creek State Park.

Trail Sense: The trails are unmarked and no map is available but orienting yourself to the rivers and roads should prevent any confusion.

Dog Friendliness
Dogs are permitted throughout the refuge.
Traffic
Seldom crowded but keep an eye out for horses and mountain bikers.
Canine Swimming
The shallow Brandywine Creek deepens enough in several places to form excellent swimming holes for dogs.
Trail Time
Whatever your dog desires - short, spirited hikes or long, long romps.

To err is human, to forgive, canine.
-Anonymous

The 50 Best Places To Hike With Your Dog Around Philadelphia...

New Jersey

Batona Trail

The Park

The *Batona Trail* is a wilderness trail that begins at Ongs Hat to the north and ends at Lake Absegami in Bass River State Forest. The original 30 miles of the *Batona Trail* were routed and cleared through white cedar and pitch pine forests by volunteers in 1961.

Today the total length of the trail is 50.2 miles with many road crossings that make different lengths of canine hikes possible. The distinctive pink blazes on the *Batona Trail* were selected by Morris Burdock, then president of the Batona Hiking Club and chief advocate for the building of the trail.

Burlington County

Phone Number
- None

Website
- None

Admission Fee
- None

Directions
- The trail runs through Lebanon, Wharton and Bass River State Forests where information on finding a parking lot can be found. Some commonly used starting points are on Routes 563 at Evans Bridge, 542 at Batsto Village at Route 72 at Four Mile.

The Walks

The *Batona Trail* is easy walking on paw-friendly sand for most of its length. Despite the over-whelming flatness of the surrounding countryside, there are undulating elevation changes on the trail itself. Any dog could walk end to end with no problem, if that was the goal.

The high point on the trail is Apple Pie Hill, soaring 209 feet above sea level (there is a fire tower you can scale - the steps are too open for dogs - and literally scan the east-to-west entirety of New Jersey from Atlantic City to Philadelphia). A superb canine hike is the four-mile walk here from the Carranza Memorial.

For the most part, however, there are no vistas beyond what you see around you - cedar swamps and millions of pine trees. In season wild blue-

Bonus

Emilio Carranza Rodriguez was nephew to the founder of the Mexican Air Force, a war hero and his country's greatest aviator. He befriended Charles Lindbergh after the American completed the first solo flight across the Atlantic and then made the second longest non-stop flight from Washington D.C. to Mexico City. Plans were hatched in 1928 for a Mexican capital-to- capital flight. Carranza, then just 22 years old, was selected to make the attempt, carrying the pride of an entire nation in his plane, "The Excelsior." Haunted by bad weather Carranza was forced to navigate by dead reckoning and came down in an emergency landing in North Carolina.
He continued on to Washington and New York City, where he was feted as a hero for accomplishing the longest flight ever made by a Mexican aviator. Preparations for a return flight to Mexico City were continually delayed until Carranza could wait no longer. On the evening of July 12 he took off in an electrical storm and was never seen alive again. The next day his body was found near the wreckage of his plane, "The Excelsior," in the Pine Barrens where he crashed. Mexican schoolchildren collected pennies to pay for the stone monument that marks the location of his death.
Post 11 of the American Legion from Mount Holly, whose members participated in the recovery of the body, still hold a memorial service every year on the second Saturday of July at 1:00 p.m. to honor the memory of Captain Emilio Carranza.

berries and huckleberries can be gobbled along the trail.

Trail Sense: The trail is generously marked with the pink blazes and a five-section trail map is available with a mileage table.

Dog Friendliness

Dogs are allowed to enjoy the *Batona Trail*.

Traffic

No horses or mountain bikes are allowed on the *Batona Trail*.

Canine Swimming

The route of the trail is well-lubricated by tea-colored streams and an occasional pond.

Trail Time

Open-ended, up to a full day, or several days.

Crow's Woods

The Park

The area was first settled in 1682 but things didn't really get going until 21-year old Elizabeth Haddon arrived in 1701 to establish her father's claims here. It wasn't until 1875 that Haddonfield Borough was officially established and the natural area south of town has been known as Crow's Woods for nearly as long. For years part of the area was used as a landfill which was converted into playing fields following the 1967 construction of the PATCO Hi-Speed Line which abuts the park. Today, the grounds at Crow's Woods encompass more than 65 acres.

Burlington County

Phone Number
- None

Website
- None

Admission Fee
- None

Directions
- *Haddonfield*; from King's Highway West head towards the Hi-Speed Line overpass and make a left on Warwick Road. After one mile make a left onto Upland Way and make a right just past the underpass into the park. Follow the park road to the end.

The Walks

Crow's Woods packs plenty of topographical diversity into its short, intermingling trails. In fact, so many dog walkers have come from outside Haddonfield to enjoy the park's ravines and hills that borough commissioners have considered imposing a "use tag" system similar to New Jersey beaches.

The wide, soft dirt paths wind through dense woodlands of scrub oak, pitch pine and mountain laurel. An asphalt jogging track around the perimeter of the sports fields is also available.

Trail Sense: Three trails are blazed in blue, yellow and white but any route can be improvised in the compact Crow's Woods without fear of becoming lost.

Bonus

Also in Haddonfield, in the north end of the borough, is the heavily wooded Pennypacker Park where dinosaur bones were discovered in 1838 in a steep ravine carved by the Cooper River. When a full excavation was initiated by William Parker Foulke in 1858 nearly 50 bones of a plant-eating, duck-billed dinosaur were discovered. Haddonfield was suddenly famous as the site of the most complete dinosaur skeleton ever found. A small memorial marks the spot where *Hadrosaurus Foulkii* was unearthed at the end of Maple Street.

Not all the trees in Crow's Woods remain standing.

Dog Friendliness
Dogs are permitted off leash in the woods but must be restrained near the playing fields.

Traffic
In addition to dog walkers, Crow's Woods is popular with mountain bikers.

Canine Swimming
There are small swimming holes in the woods that are more suited for a refreshing splash than sustained dog paddling.

Trail Time
Less than one hour.

Fort Mott State Park

The Park

Fort Mott was envisioned as part of a three-fort defense of Philadelphia that dangled across the Delaware River. Following the Civil War, work began on 11 gun emplacements but only two were completed when the fort was abandoned in 1876. In preparation for the Spanish-American War in 1896, Fort Mott, named to honor Major General Gershom Mott, a native of Bordentown, was completed and outfitted with three 10-inch and three 12-inch guns. The fort remained active until 1943, although during its last two decades the guns were dismantled and shipped elsewhere. In 1947 the State of New Jersey purchased Fort Mott as an historic site and opened the state park on June 24, 1951.

New Castle County

Phone Number
- (609) 935-3218

Website
- state.nj.us/dep/forestry/parks/fortmot.htm

Admission Fee
- None

Directions
- *Pennsville*; from Exit 1 of I-295, take Route 49 East to Fort Mott Road. Turn right onto Fort Mott Road and travel three miles. Park is located on right.

The Walks

Fort Mott features a walking tour through the 19th century defensive position that enables your dog to ramble through the gun batteries and ammunition magazines and to clamber on top of the massive protective parapet. This concrete wall was built of concrete poured 35 feet thick with an additional 60 feet of earth piled in front. Landscaping made the fort look like a big hill from the Delaware River.

In additon to this unique dog walk there is a groomed trail that winds through twelve-foot high swamp grasses to Finn's Point National Cemetery, the final resting place for 2,436 Confederate soldiers who perished in a Civil War prisoner of war camp at Fort Delaware.

Trail Sense: A map of the walking tour of is available.

Bonus
Where else can your dog climb into an actual battery and scan the Delaware River where gunnery officers once aimed guns capable of accurately firing 1,000-pound projectiles eight miles?

Your dog will love the sandy beach and frisky Delaware River waves at Fort Mott State Park.

Dog Friendliness
Dogs are permitted in the state park.

Traffic
Not many people make their way to this remote outpost on the banks of the Delaware River.

Canine Swimming
Fort Mott State Park is the closest thing to an ocean swimming experience in the Delaware Valley. Below the ferry pier is a sand beach with enough wave action to convince your dog he's chasing that stick into the Atlantic.

Trail Time
About an hour, depending on how much time you spend on the beach.

"Any man who does not like dogs and want them does not deserve to be in the White House."
-Calvin Coolidge

Parvin
State Park

The Park

The first landowner of these diverse pinelands was John Estaugh, husband of Elizabeth Haddon, who lived in present-day Haddonfield. Estaugh was granted 2,928 acres on March 31, 1742, by the Proprietors of West Jersey. Development began in 1796 when Lemuel Parvin purchased the property with the intention of operating a sawmill. He created Parvin Lake by constructing an earthen dam across Muddy Run on its journey to the Maurice River.

Salem County

Phone Number
- (609) 358-8616

Website
- state.nj.us/dep/
forestry/parks/parvin.htm

Admission Fee
- None

Directions
- *Vineland*; six miles west of town on Route 540, just east of the intersection with Route 553.

The State of New Jersey's stewardship began in 1930 with the acquisition of 918 acres of forest and the 108-acre lake. During the Depression of the 1930s the Civilian Conservation Corps established a camp at Parvin, building campgrounds and cabins and carving trails. In 1944, German prisoners of war from Fort Dix were housed in Parvin while working on local farms and food processing plants. The POWS were captured from German Field Marshall Erwin Rommell's marauding Afrika Corps. Many of the facilities built by the Civilian Conservation Corps are still in use in the park today.

The Walks

A variety of loops and linear trails slice across Parvin State Park's 1,135 acres, about evenly divided between a recreational area and a natural area. The canine hiking is easier in the recreational area with its wide, packed-sand trails; paths narrow in the oak-pine forests, cedar swamps and laurel thickets of the natural area. These scenic woodlands on the fringe of the Pine Barrens are home to 40 known types of trees and 61 different woody shrubs as southern United States ecosystems collide with northern species at the

> *Bonus*
> **For the dog who favors entering the water with a well-executed belly flop there are boat docks available, including a wide wooden pier stretching 25 yards into Lake Parvin for Dock Diving practice.**

southern tip of their natural range. All the hiking with your dog is on nine named trails, totalling more than 15 miles, and is easy-going for any dog.

Trail Sense: Only trailheads on the major trails are marked and trail blazes disappear in the natural area. Don't let go of the park map on long hikes.

Dog Friendliness

All trails are open to dogs but they are not permitted in the campgrounds and cabins and in the Parvin Grove beach area.

Traffic

This is not a heavily used park and away from the campgrounds and picnic groves isolation can be realized. Only a few trails are hiker-only, however.

Canine Swimming

There is excellent doggie paddling in the attractive Parvin Lake and there is abundant access to the water in smaller Thundergast Lake. Although access is limited, the swimming is also good in the deceptively-named Muddy Run.

Trail Time

Several hours of canine hiking are on the menu here.

Washington Crossing State Park

The Park

These sleepy, tree-lined banks along the Delaware River became immortalized in American mythology on the icy night of December 25, 1776 when General George Washington led a demoralized Continental Army across the river to score a surprise victory over unsuspecting Hessian troops in Trenton.

Land was eventually preserved on both the New Jersey and Pennsylvania sides of the river to commemorate one of the turning points in the battle for independence.

Mercer County

Phone Number
- (609) 737-0623

Website
- state.nj.us/dep/forestry/parks/washcros.htm

Admission Fee
- None

Directions
- *Titusville*; from I-95, take Route 29 north. Parking is available along the Delaware River just past Route 546.

The Walks

There are dog-walking opportunities on both sides of the Delaware; the more historic explorations can be found on the Pennsylvania side, the more natural trails in New Jersey. Quiet paths meander through an historic village at the scene of the American disembarkment in Washington's Crossing Historic Park.

On the New Jersey side, the terrain instantly becomes rolling and wooded beyond the Johnson Ferry House where the troops landed in what is now Washington Crossing State Park. The many miles of trails are carved through a mixed hardwood and spruce forest, often times plunging into and out of wide ravines.

Washington Crossing State Park can also be used as a jumping off point for hikes up and down the towpath along the 70-mile Delaware and Raritan Canal.

Trail Sense: The trails are not blazed and maps are not available.

Bonus
You can trace the route of Washington's troops with your dog by walking across the Delaware River on a steel bridge. The bridge affords long views of the river as well.

Maybe Washington's troops rested here as well.

Dog Friendliness

Dogs can enjoy the New Jersey trails and on the Pennsylvania side look at the outside of buildings in Washington Crossing Historic Park's McConkey's Ferry Section. Dogs are not allowed in Bowman's Hill Wildflower Preserve upstream in the Thompson's Mill Section on the Pennsylvania side.

Traffic

The towpath is popular with joggers and bicyclists but the crowds thin out on the hills of the state park.

Canine Swimming

There is no good access to the Delaware River at this point.

Trail Time

More than an hour, especially if you set off on the towpath.

"The greatest pleasure of a dog is that you may make a fool of yourself with him, and not only will he not scold you, but will make a fool of himself too."

- Samuel Butler

Wenonah Woods

The Park

Wenonah grew out of a resort community that was founded in 1872, carved from the surrounding Deptford area. It was later the location of a junior-high and high-school level military academy, until the late 1930s. Interconnected wooded trails loop around the southern half of the town from northwest to east.

The Walks

From the north, across from Wenonah Lake, the first trail is *Break Back Run*, winding along wooded stream valleys and ridges. Next is the *Clay Hill Trail* where the walking is level save for the namesake hill by a bend in the stream.

The well-maintained *Glen Trail* connects the paths on both sides of the railroad. A brief side trail to Clinton Street leads to a tiny, stone fish pond, a quaint remnant of Wenonah's 19th century resort days. Continuing onto the *George Eldridge Trail*, the path features many streams and wooden bridges.

Side trails lead to more hiking on the *Deptford/Sewell Trails* and the *Monongahela Brook Trail*, a half-mile loop that rolls along the south shore and drops to a flat creekside return trip. Some of the biggest trees in the Wenonah Woods can be found here.

The last trail is *Covey's Lake Trail*, a 3/4-mile loop along the quiet tree-lined shore. The lake was once a center for leisurely recreation at the resort, sporting a boathouse and a teahouse. Watch for snakes in the rocks around the lake.

Trail Sense: No blazes but wooden posts at trail junctions.

Burlington County

Phone Number
- None

Website
- oocities.org/woodsofwenonah/

Admission Fee
- None

Directions
- *Wenonah*; on Route 553. The trails are accessed from several points around town including Hayes Road at East Mantua Avenue; the west end of West Cedar Street; and the east end of Pine Street.

An elaborate, reinforced wooden railroad trestle bridges a ravine on the Glen Trail. The trail runs by a stream under the trestle and there are sweeping views of Wenonah Woods from the top.

Sometimes getting into the ponds in Wenonah Woods is easier than getting out.

Dog Friendliness
Dogs are welcome along all the trails here.

Traffic
There are backyards every 15 minutes or so but not much competition on the trails.

Canine Swimming
At the northern terminus of *Break Back Run Trail*, across North Jefferson Avenue is Davidson's Lake, a super canine swimming hole. Comey's Lake is algae-encrusted but there is access to clear water near the wooden dock.

Trail Time
More than an hour.

"Dogs' lives are too short. Their only fault, really."
-Agnes Sligh Turnbull

Wharton State Forest

The Park

Wharton State Forest lies at the heart of New Jersey's mysterious Pine Barrens, a tapestry of impenetrable scrub pine, swamps and bogs. Today known for its cranberry and blueberry production, the area's bog ore once supported a booming iron industry which supplied much of the weaponry for the American Revolution. Many of the indecipherable sand roads through the Pine Barrens date to that time.

When the foundries followed the discovery of America's massive upper midwestern iron ranges in the mid-1800s, the area's economy became so depressed that Philadelphia financier Joseph Wharton was able to acquire over 100,000 acres of land here. That land now makes up the state forest - the largest single tract of land in the New Jersey state park system.

Burlington County

Phone Number
- (609) 561-0024

Website
- state.nj.us/dep/forestry/parks/wharton.htm

Admission Fee
- Parking fee charged weekends in season at Batsto

Directions
- Wharton State Forest has two offices: at Batsto Village on Route 542, eight miles east of Hammonton, and at Atsion Recreation Area on Route 206, eight miles north of Hammonton.

The Walks

The main hiking trail through Wharton State Forest is the *Batona Trail* but for dogs who feel cramped by the rigidness of a narrow 50-mile band there are more than 500 miles of unpaved sand roads in Wharton State Forest.

If that is too much choice, bring your dog to Batsto Village. Thirty-three wooden structures have been restored to this bog iron and glassmaking industrial center which flourished from 1766 to 1867. There is a self-guided one-mile nature walk around the lake at Batsto Village, that includes stops at the Batsto Mansion and an operating gristmill and sawmill.

Trail Sense: Off the *Batona Trail* you are own your own - do you want to map 500 miles of roads?

Bonus

The chance to see New Jersey's version of Bigfoot, the legendary winged creature known as the "Jersey Devil." The Jersey Devil is a creature with the head of a horse supported by a four-foot serpentine body with large wings and claws. According to lore, the Devil appeared in the 1700s when an indigent woman named Mrs. Leeds was struggling to feed her twelve children in the darkest recesses of the Pine Barrens. Finding herself once again pregnant she is said to have exclaimed: "I want no more children! Let it be a devil." The devil-child was born horribly deformed, crawled from the womb, up the chimney and into the woods where it was rumored to survive by feeding on small children and livestock, haunting the countryside. When a person saw the Devil, it was an omen of disaster, particularly shipwrecks, to come. Sightings were common through the next two centuries and often breathlessly reported in the local newspapers. Once some local Pineys, as Pine Barrens residents are known, tried to claim a $10,000 reward for capturing the Devil by obtaining a kangaroo, painting stripes across its back and gluing large wings on the animal. But so no documented Jersey Devils have been captured. Perhaps your dog can sniff one out.

Dog Friendliness

Dogs are welcome across Wharton State Forest.

Traffic

Most of the trails in Wharton State Forest are unimproved dirt roads that hikers share with on-and off-road vehicles. But don't be surprised if you never see anyone.

Canine Swimming

An aquifer inside the Pine Barren's deep sand beds holds 17 trillion gallons of pure glacial water. The shallow aquifer often percolates to the surface in the form of bogs, marshes and swamps. The slow-moving Batsto River is stained the color of tea by cedar sap, adding to the region's mystique. It makes an excellent canine swimming pool - or a wonderful water trail in a canoe.

Trail Time

Many hours - or days - are possible on these trails.

Your Dog At The Beach

It is hard to imagine many places a dog is happier than at a beach. Whether running around on the sand, jumping in the water or just lying in the sun, every dog deserves a day at the beach. But all too often dog owners stopping at a sandy stretch of beach are met with signs designed to make hearts - human and canine alike - droop: NO DOGS ON BEACH. Below are rules for taking your dog on a day trip to one of our Atlantic Ocean beaches.

Delaware

Off-season, Delaware's quiet, sandy beaches area a paradise for dogs. Dogs can also play in the summer waves at Delaware Seashore State Park.

Bethany Beach	No dogs on the beach or boardwalk from April 1 to October 1
Delaware Seashore State Park	Dogs are allowed on the beach from October 1 to May 1 and selected beaches year-round
Dewey Beach	Dogs are not allowed on the beach between 9:30 am to 5:30 pm in season
Fenwick Island	No dogs permitted on the beach from May 1 to September 30
Lewes/ Cape Henlopen	From May 1 to September 30 no dogs are allowed on the beach between 8:00 am and 6:30 pm
Rehoboth Beach	Dogs are prohibited from the beach and boardwalk from April 1 to October 31

Maryland

The drive is a little longer but if you want your dog to enjoy the ocean waves in the summer the place to go is Assateague Island National Seashore.

Assateague Island National Seashore	Dogs are allowed on the beach but not on the trails year-round
Assateague State Park	No dogs are allowed on the beach
Ocean City	Dogs are allowed on the beach and boardwalk October 1 to April 30

New Jersey

In-season, the New Jersey shore isn't especially welcoming to canine hikers. After Labor Day, however, some of America's best sand beaches start to open wide for dogs.

Asbury Park	Dogs are allowed on beach in off-season
Atlantic City	Dogs are not permitted on the beaches or boardwalk anytime
Avalon	Dogs are not permitted on the beach, boardwalk or dunes between March 1 and September 30
Avon-By-The-Sea	Dogs allowed on beach from November 1 to April 1 but never on the boardwalk
Barnegat Light	Dogs are prohibited from May 1 to October 1
Beach Haven	No dogs allowed on the beach
Belmar	Dogs are not allowed on the beach

Bonus

While dogs are banned from most of the popular Victorian town of Cape May, our four-legged friends are welcome at Sunset Beach at the southernmost point on Cape May. Just off the beach are the remains of the Atlantus, a unique concrete ship built to transport soldiers in World War I. With steel at a shortage, reinforced concrete was tried as a shipbuilding material. The concrete ships worked but proved too slow and were scrapped after the war. The Atlantus was towed to Cape May in 1926 to be used as a Ferry slip but an accident dumped her on a sand bar where she remains today. From the center of Cape May take Lafayette Avenue to West Perry Street, which turns into Sunset Boulevard. The two-lane road deadends after three miles at Sunset Beach.

Bradley Beach	Dogs are allowed from October 15 to April 15
Brigantine	Dogs are allowed on the beach from 14th Street north to the northernmost jetty
Cape May	Dogs are not allowed on the beach, board walk or outdoor shopping areas
Cape May Point	No dogs allowed on the beach
Gateway National Recreation Area - Sandy Hook	Dogs allowed on the beach from Labor Day to March 15
Island Beach State Park	Dogs are not allowed in recreational areas but have access to other beaches any time of the year
Lavallette	No dogs allowed on beach but can go on boardwalk after Labor Day

Mantoloking	Dogs allowed on the beach October 1 to May 15 anytime; otherwise dogs allowed from sunrise to 8 AM and 6 PM to sunset
North Wildwood	Dogs are not allowed on the beach from May 15 to September 15

Sometimes good sticks are hard to find on the open dunes of Island Beach State Park.

Ocean City	Dogs are never allowed on the boardwalk but can be leashed on the beach from October 1 to April 30
Ocean Grove	Dogs are permitted on the beach and boardwalk from October 1 to May 1
Point Pleasant	Dogs allowed anytime from September 15 until June 15; before 8:00 AM and after 6:00 PM in the summer

Sea Isle City	No dogs are permitted on the beach, beach approaches or promenade at any time
Ship Bottom	No dogs allowed on the beach until October 1
Spring Lake	Dogs are allowed on the beach in the off-season
Stone Harbor	No dogs allowed on the beach, boardwalk or dunes anytime between March 1 and September 30
Surf City	No dogs allowed on the beach
Wildwood	No dogs allowed on the beach
Wildwood Crest	No animals of any kind allowed on the beach

Dogs are never at a loss for things to do at the beach.

Tips For Taking Your Dog To The Beach

- The majority of dogs can swim and love it, but dogs entering the water for the first time should be tested; never throw a dog into the water. Start in shallow water and call your dog's name - or try to coax him in with a treat or toy. Always keep your dog within reach.

- Another way to introduce your dog to the water is with a dog that already swims and is friendly with your dog. Let your dog follow his friend.

- If your dog begins to doggie paddle with his front legs only, lift his hind legs and help him float. He should quickly catch on and will keep his back end up.

- Swimming is a great form of exercise, but don't let your dog overdo it. He will be using new muscles and may tire quickly.

- Be careful of strong tides that are hazardous for even the best swimmers.

- Cool ocean water is tempting to your dog. Do not allow him to drink too much sea water. Salt in the water will make him sick. Salt and other minerals found in the ocean can damage your dog's coat so regular bathing is essential.

- Check with a lifeguard for daily water conditions - dogs are easy targets for jellyfish and sea lice.

- Dogs can get sunburned, especially short-haired dogs and ones with pink skin and white hair. Limit your dog's exposure when the sun is strong and apply sunblock to his ears and nose 30 minutes before going outside.

- If your dog is out of shape, don't encourage him to run on the sand, which is strenuous exercise and a dog that is out of shape can easily pull a tendon or ligament.

Index to Delaware Valley Parks By State

Pennsylvania   page

Anson B. Nixon Park   18
Darlington Trail   20
Evansburg State Park   22
Fairmount Park-Andorra Natural Area   24
French Creek State Park   26
Green Lane Park   28
Heinz National Wildlife Refuge   30
Hibernia County Park   32
Indian Orchard/Linvill Trails   34
Lorimer Nature Preserve   36
Marsh Creek State Park   38
McKaig Nature Education Center   40
Monocacy Hill   42
Neshaminy State Park   44
Norristown Farm Park   46
Nottingham County Park   48
Nockamixon State Park   50
Oakbourne Park   52
Pennypack Park   54
Pennypack Preserve   56
Ralph Stover/Tohickon Valley Park   58
Ridley Creek State Park   60
Riverbend Education Center   62
Schuylkill Canal Park   64
Scott Arboretum   66
Springfield Trail   68
Springton Manor Park   70
State Game Lands #43   72
Tamanend Community Park   74
Taylor Arboretum   76
Tyler State Park   78
Valley Forge National Historic Park   80
Warwick County Park   82
Welkinweir   84

Delaware page

Alapocas Woods State Park	88
Ashland Nature Center	90
Bellevue State Park	92
Brandywine Creek State Park	94
Carousel Park	96
Middle Run Valley Natural Area	98
White Clay Creek State Park/Preserve	100
Wilmington State Parks	102
Woodlawn Trustees Property	104

New Jersey page

Batona Trail	108
Crow's Woods	110
Fort Mott State Park	112
Parvin State Park	114
Washington Crossing State Park	116
Wenonah Woods	118
Wharton State Forest	120

"I can't think of anything that brings me closer to tears than when my old dog - completely exhausted afters a hard day in the field - limps away from her nice spot in front of the fire and comes over to where I'm sitting and puts her head in my lap, a paw over my knee, and closes her eyes, and goes back to sleep. I don't know what I've done to deserve that kind of friend."
-Gene Hill

Other Books On Hiking With Your Dog from Cruden Bay Books
www.hikewithyourdog.com

DOGGIN' AMERICA: 100 Ideas For Great Vacations To Take With Your Dog - $19.95

DOGGIN' THE MID-ATLANTIC: 400 Tail-Friendly Parks To Hike With Your Dog In New Jersey, Pennsylvania, Delaware, Maryland and Northern Virginia - $18.95

DOGGIN' CLEVELAND: The 50 Best Places To Hike With Your Dog In Northeast Ohio - $12.95

DOGGIN' PITTSBURGH: The 50 Best Places To Hike With Your Dog In Southeast Pennsylvania - $12.95

DOGGIN' ORLANDO: The 30 Best Places To Hike With Your Dog in Central Florida - $9.95

DOGGIN' NORTHWEST FLORIDA: The 50 Best Places To Hike With Your Dog In The Panhandle - $12.95

DOGGIN' ATLANTA: The 50 Best Places To Hike With Your Dog in North Georgia - $12.95

DOGGIN' THE POCONOS: The 33 Best Places To Hike With Your Dog In Pennsylvania's Northeast Mountains - $9.95

DOGGIN' THE BERKSHIRES: The 33 Best Places To Hike With Your Dog In Western Massachusetts - $9.95

DOGGIN' NORTHERN VIRGINIA: The 50 Best Places To Hike With Your Dog In NOVA - $9.95

DOGGIN' DELAWARE: The 40 Best Places To Hike With Your Dog In The First State - $9.95

DOGGIN' MARYLAND: The 100 Best Places To Hike With Your Dog In The Free State - $12.95

DOGGIN' JERSEY: The 100 Best Places To Hike With Your Dog In The Garden State - $12.95

DOGGIN' RHODE ISLAND: The 25 Best Places To Hike With Your Dog In The Ocean State - $7.95

DOGGIN' MASSACHUSETTS: The 100 Best Places To Hike With Your Dog in the Bay State - $12.95

DOGGIN' CONNECTICUT: The 57 Best Places To Hike With Your Dog In The Nutmeg State - $12.95

DOGGIN' THE FINGER LAKES: The 50 Best Places To Hike With Your Dog - $12.95

DOGGIN' LONG ISLAND: The 30 Best Places To Hike With Your Dog In New York's Playground - $9.95

DOGGIN' THE TIDEWATER: The 33 Best Places To Hike With Your Dog from the Northern Neck to Virginia Beach - $9.95

DOGGIN' THE CAROLINA COASTS: The 50 Best Places To Hike With Your Dog Along The North Carolina And South Carolina Shores - $11.95

DOGGIN' AMERICA'S BEACHES: A Traveler's Guide To Dog-Friendly Beaches - $12.95

THE CANINE HIKER'S BIBLE - $19.95

DOOGIN' ASHEVILLE: The 50 Best Places To Hike With Your Dog In The Blue Ridge - $12.95

A Bark In The Park: The 50 Best Places To Hike With Your Dog In The Baltimore Region - $12.95

A Bark In The Park: The 37 Best Places To Hike With Your Dog In Pennsylvania Dutch Country - $9.95

www.ingramcontent.com/pod-product-compliance
Lightning Source LLC
Chambersburg PA
CBHW060514030426
42337CB00015B/1888